GO!

A Journey of Surrender and Trust

Doug Sprague

purposequest
INK

GO!
by Doug Sprague
Copyright ©2016 Doug Sprague

ISBN 978-1-63360-053-9
For Worldwide Distribution

Printed in the U.S.A.

PurposeQuest Ink
P.O. Box 8882
Pittsburgh, PA 15221-0882
412.646.2780

To my dad, who, many years ago, invested so many hours teaching me to write and who became the biggest fan of my work at Bongolo. I love you always and all ways!

- Doug

Table of Contents

Foreword

The book you hold in your hands, *Go! A Journey of Surrender and Trust*, is a transparently personal yet universal book. Doug Sprague has captured in words the process that so many of us go through in our search to follow God. In his case, it led to a remote jungle hospital called Bongolo. Your search may take you somewhere else, though I am sure you will identify with Doug's journey, for it is really the journey that each one of us is on. His stories of God's leading, protection, and guidance, and Doug's accounts of his denial of self and submission to a higher call, all resonate with all of us, since they are part of our human pilgrimage here on earth. It is what we all struggle to live and seek to experience.

Doug's landing zone was Bongolo Hospital. Founded in 1977 on the heels of a fruitful spiritual ministry to the southern part of French Equatorial Africa, Bongolo Hospital continues to be a place where people of all backgrounds meet God, some for the first time, while others encounter him on a daily basis. Whether patients or staff are Gabonese, American, Congolese, Malian, Cameroonian, Guinean, or Nigerian, Bongolo Hospital provides a place of hope and healing for everyone. Bongolo's presence in the tropical rainforest is truly a light in the dark. People who come are hurting, most of them physically, but almost all are hurting spiritually. Bongolo is a source of healing through both medical and spiritual care delivered by generalists, pediatricians, family medicine, obstetricians, surgeons, and ophthalmologists. Most importantly, all of the staff provide spiritual care to these hurting people.

As you see Bongolo through Doug's eyes, you will be confronted with the challenges of living in such a rainforest. You may be inspired to consider if God is guiding your journey to a place like Bongolo. We can all identify with Doug as he shares how his stubbornness and personal agenda took him to the brink of exhaustion spiritually and physically. Then you will learn how God meets him, opens a door, and reminds Doug that it is really all about Him.

These truly are God's stories as told through Doug. His accounts will bring you to the remotest Africa, face-to-face with a new world, a world that once seemed so far away to Doug, but one that will draw near as you immerse yourself in the journal accounts of his time before, during, and after his trip to Bongolo. His honesty teaches many valuable lessons, and reveals the heart of a man broken and remade for the work God has for him.

Open your own heart as you read, and be challenged by the stories told and lessons learned. I must warn you to be careful, for this book will cause you to rethink how, where, and why you follow God. It will open your mind to a new world, one where God wants to live and breathe in and through you, and that may not be where you are serving Him at the present moment. I promise, however, that you will not regret taking this journey with Doug to the jungle of Africa. Enjoy the ride, and may the Lord speak to your heart as you go!

Dr. Keir Thelander

Chief Medical Officer — Pan-African Academy of Christian Surgeons (PAACS)

Medical Director, Surgeon, and Team Leader at Bongolo Hospital (until 2015)

Who am *I* to Write a Book?

My two-month trip to Bongolo Hospital, which is chronicled in these pages, was, to a great extent, a journey to figure out whether or not God wanted me in the mission field on a full-time basis. Before leaving for Africa, I had determined to write a blog about my experiences and what I learned because, over the years, I've found that writing helps me to think through important things more deeply. When my good friend, mentor, and now publisher, John Stanko, suggested that this blog would make a good book concept, I politely nodded, expressed my thanks, and told him I would think about it. "After all," I thought, "John thinks everything would make a good book!" While I was intrigued by the idea, I had been disappointed that three other books I had written have not yet made it all the way to the printer.

"Why would this one be any different?" I thought.

At the same time, I love to write. I've regularly blogged for years and now have hundreds of posts communicating the power of faith-filled, positive affirmations for personal growth and life transformation. Writing these not only allowed me to share what I had learned with others, it also helped solidify those lessons in my own mind. Friends have encouraged me to turn those posts into two books, but I've never felt released or inclined to do so. It's not that I didn't think it wouldn't be worthwhile, I just didn't believe the time was right. Similarly, I've written most of a business book about my sales and life-coaching methodology, mixed with stories of my growth as a salesperson. That's not yet gone to the publisher, either. So, questions remained: Would I ever publish? Should I?

After I had posted several entries the first week at Bongolo, however, I began to sense this book effort might be different. The responses were overwhelmingly supportive and more people connected with them than with anything I had previously written. "Maybe John has something, after all," I thought. John also weighed in and encouraged me to keep writing and see what happened, so I did.

It's important to clarify that, while I'm the main voice throughout the book, this effort really isn't about me. It's about God continuing to teach one normal guy to surrender to and trust his Lord's promptings in all areas of his life and culminating in, as of now, a life-changing extended mission trip to the jungle of Africa. While you do get to know me a little bit in this book, my intent is that your attention instead be on what I've learned, and how that might impact you as you seek and pursue God's will for your life.

As you'll find out, this was truly God's trip. It is also *His* book. I prayerfully hope God somehow uses what I've learned so far to help you as you seek His will for your own future, or to confirm and act upon what you've already sensed from Him.

"Go"

Huh? What? I didn't hear an actual voice that wintery day in 2015, but it was definitely a God connection. While I've been a Christian much of my life and had become familiar with His promptings, I had never sensed actual words before that particular moment. To be honest, it was a little weird. In the past, God had gotten His points across to me through the Bible, other people, clearly laid out paths to a decision, and even with humor! For years, I've been working on more quickly discerning when a message, sense, or a prompting is from Him, and then to more and more quickly surrender, trust, and act. Even though this was different, I pretty quickly understood "Go" as my latest opportunity to give God more and more control over my life.

That's not to say that this "lifestyle of obedience" was easily obtained. Like many others, it's taken much of my life to learn God's blessings that come by following His ways far outweigh the perceived costs. Rock Dillaman, my pastor for more than 25 years, preached about this truth from the pulpit a while back. He basically said that the things of God usually appear to be restrictive and painful in the short run, but, over time, *always* lead to amazing results. The contrast is that the things of this world are always incredibly appealing in the short run — sin is like that — but the consequences of pursuing those things always end up being empty and void of meaning. I've experienced enough of each of these results from pursuing God and my own desires, and, although still far from mastery, I now completely agree with Rock.

It hasn't always that way. I'm generally considered to be a stand up kind of guy — somebody people turn to in times of need for advice, support, or a shoulder to cry on. Maybe that's the coach in me, I don't know. But, I'm also an independent, *stubborn*, and strong-willed sinner filled with rebellion, disobedience, and pride that still try to take over. Maybe that's how you are as well. Regardless, it's important for me to communicate that learning to quickly obey has taken me a lifetime to achieve, and it's been a journey full of ups and downs. I would be a fool to think that, in spite of my best efforts, I won't fall short sometime today, let alone in the future. It's taken a lot of patient effort on God's part to train me to pay attention to Him. So, this prompting to "go" was not one that I was either going to ignore or fail to pursue. Now all I needed to do was to find out where.

Early Promptings

When I look over my life and reflect, it's clear God had been attempting to get through to me for years. The earliest awareness of some kind of "prompting" from Him was during the first few years of having my driver's license. Boy, God, it sure took me a long time to catch on. You see, once I got out on my own, I pretty quickly became an aggressive driver. Let's just say that I acquired too many speeding tickets for my checkbook to handle, but somehow avoided losing my license. For some reason, I was consumed by the desire to "win" by driving faster than the other drivers, and couldn't stand to feel constrained behind a slow-moving vehicle when the open road ahead was calling me. Therefore, I passed as often as possible.

Back then, I had a rural sales territory and most of my driving was on rural two-lane roads. Over time, I began to notice an unusual but consistent gut feeling every time I went to pass the car in front of me. If it was safe, I'd sense a release to go, so I did. But, if it was dangerous, there was always this unnerving "No!" sensation as well. In spite of this, I often attempted to pass. It didn't matter what time of day or what the weather was. I passed way too often in dangerous conditions that easily could have caused accidents. I regularly scared the daylights out of myself and, I'm sure, other drivers.

Fortunately, I was never in a speed-related accident. Unfortunately, I was a very immature Christian, and it never occurred to me that it was God protecting me from myself. I finally caught on to the pattern, however. Obeying it probably saved my life and the lives of others many times over. For some reason, I never told anybody about them. I guess some of that was pride, as well as a healthy fear of being laughed at, but mostly it was because I forgot about them as soon as I got wherever I was headed. Regardless of the reason, I lost the opportunity for somebody to speak wisdom into my life. I just wish I'd known back then that it was God reaching out to me.

A second way God would communicate with me was in my work life. I grew up wanting to be the president of a company. I was quite ambitious and worked hard to make that a reality. God had other plans, however, and in 1992, I decided to obey what I now realize was His prompting to instead become a better "president" of my family as best I could. A few years earlier, my wife had become physically disabled when our two children were still very young. So, I found myself working full time, driving the kids to and from their Christian school, while doing my best to care for my wife. It took me a while to accept that I couldn't do all that was needed at home and also become a successful businessman. In exhaustion, I finally accepted that I was not put here on Earth to do all I could to earn the money I was capable of earning. Instead, I was supposed to focus on service to those God gave me to care for.

Tragically, my wife and I parted ways several years later, and I thought that service assignment would have been lifted after the divorce was final, but it wasn't. I tried to pursue money and success even after the divorce, but they still weren't what God wanted for me. That's been a tough pill for this ambitious type-A personality to accept, but I have. While there have been a lot of difficult financial times since then, as well as numerous crises brought on through pride and envy, I'm glad I listened and obeyed. Ironically, over the last fifteen years, I did eventually found and run four companies, one with about twenty construction workers and four office staff. So, I guess you could say that I accomplished my youthful goal to be president of a company, just not the way I thought it would happen. God wanted me to focus on growing with Him, instead of focusing on the marketplace. In spite of fits and starts, my trust that He knew what He was doing continued to grow.

Dating Promptings

Driving and career promptings were actually pretty straightforward compared to how God wanted me to handle my post-divorce dating life. Since 2001, my hope has always been to remarry, but that hasn't happened as of the time of this writing! That's okay, because back in 2001, God and I made a "deal." He definitely knows (because I've told Him for years) that I desire to be remarried and stay with "her" for the rest of my life, and I'm hoping He's working on bringing this about. I've also told Him that I'd *much* rather stay single for the rest of my life than repeat my horrific past mistakes. Over time, I've (less and less) grudgingly accepted that He just might want me to stay single for the rest of my life. If that's the case, I've come to believe it is because He believes that is a better path for me and I will trust that He'll take good care of me, whatever that means. The year 2001 is now a *long* time ago and I'm still not remarried – not even close as a matter of fact.

I've dated – mostly trying to do so God's way, but frequently falling short. Obeying His instructions around my actual dating life was more difficult to accept than anything I've gone through – much harder than obeying driving and career promptings. For example, from the start of my single-again life, I aspired to sexual purity, but I'm sad to say it took me years to make that a stake-in-the-ground commitment. While this has been a big challenge, it's also been a magnificent blessing well worth the effort. I now recommend the spiritual, psychological, and emotional benefits of celibacy to everybody who asks.

Another example from dating of my being slow to learn was accepting that God only wanted me to date women who know Jesus as their Lord and Savior, no matter how fabulous they may be. It was always my intent to date only Christians, but I was pretty generous with that label. I found loophole after loophole, and it *never* worked out. God used one of my better friends to finally challenge me to stop "missionary dating." He pointed out that I'd meet a great woman, she'd become a Christian, then we'd break up, and I'd start the cycle all over again! It took a while to heed his advice, but I finally did. Talk about a sure-fire way to shrink my options! Even in a large metropolitan area like Pittsburgh, do you have any idea how difficult it is to find a local, emotionally healthy, fit, attractive, kind, available Christian woman in her 40s or early 50s, who actually likes me in return? In spite of this, I am more committed than ever to date God's way with no exceptions. Period.

One of the hardest dating lessons was the most recent that started in early 2015. At that time, I was mostly Internet dating and this one Christian site had been a source for meeting some really great women — heck, more than half of them even looked like their photos! It was then that I sensed a new prompting: *"Don't date at all."* "What? Come *on!* You've got to be kidding!" was all I could think. God, however, was dead serious — again.

Initially, I gave God the nod and wink of obedience. Translated, that means I kept doing things my way. But not too long afterwards, I started noticing changes to the online communicating patterns. It dawned on me that none of the women I'd reached out to online in the prior *month* had replied to my invitations to communicate. "That's weird," I thought. I went back into my email feed to make sure I hadn't missed somebody's message, but I had not. There were no polite refusals, let alone any "Sure!" messages. Then I checked my profile to see if somebody had hacked it and changed my photos, and that wasn't the case, either. What was going on?

At the same time, I noticed I was receiving more incoming requests to get acquainted, but *all* of them were from women in whom I wasn't interested. I monitored these trends over the next couple of weeks and the pattern was solid: No responses, and only "no way!" incoming contacts. I finally stopped reaching out to potential dates. Maybe I wasn't supposed to be dating after all.

In partial obedience, I started going to this site less and less, but every time I checked in, the results were the same, *except* for one significant change: The women contacting me progressively got less and less appealing. It eventually got so bad that I started to laugh before even opening the incoming messages. It finally dawned on me that perhaps the Creator was patiently using gentle humor to get His point across.

Finally, about a month after he told me *not* to date any more, I finally threw up my hands in submission. Laughter in God's hands is a powerful phenomenon! It was also nice that He chose to spare me from going through yet another dramatic and traumatic experience. As a result, I've had a fantastic time building friendships, taking business risks, and doing other time-consuming things that would have been more difficult to do while in a serious relationship. I have grown to be very comfortable as a single man.

By then, I was getting the hang of obeying: this time, it only took me about a month. Not that this is anything to brag about, but I was improving! That kind of awareness starts to happen when we become more in tune with God's promptings and become more sensitive to His desires — at least that's been the case in my life.

In hindsight, it's now perfectly obvious why God didn't want me to date: He was providentially clearing out any human barriers that might have gotten in the way of saying "Yes" to going to Bongolo. If I had been dating somebody, would I have still gone? I don't know, and, fortunately, I didn't have to make that decision. But I've gotten ahead of the story.

I still want to get married again, however. That desire hasn't left me.

"Go," but First Wait

All of this brings me back to the mysterious prompting to "Go." As soon as I became aware of it, I resolved that this time, I was going to do it God's way right from the beginning with no delays, no questions, and no excuses. I determined it would be straightforward trust and submission because His ways have always worked out for my best. There would be no more denseness, blatant rebellion, or learning the hard way.

So, finally, I was obeying. But, "Houston, we have a problem." Nothing seemed to be happening! I fully expected the veil to be pulled back as soon as I said I'd obey and my mission would be crystal clear. It felt like He might be talking about something international, but was that just me talking? I didn't know. There was no revelation, no "aha" breakthrough moment. Nothing.

Unbelievably, this continued for the next several *months*. For the first time in my promptings experience, I had absolutely no idea what one meant. Go where? When? Do what? Not only did I not have any answers to these questions, I also didn't even have any definitive clues.

During this time, I learned a lot more about active waiting — not an easy assignment, to say the least. I didn't think God wanted me to sit around twiddling my thumbs, so I started seeking. I had meetings with my pastors, closest friends, my coaches and mentors, and so on. Every once in a while, somebody would suggest something that sounded interesting, and I'd start exploring, but it never went anywhere. You could say I learned what *not* to pursue. It was difficult not to grasp onto something — anything — and move forward.

I even started fantasizing again about a discarded four-year-old scheme to become fluent in Spanish. Maybe, I thought, this was what God meant by "Go"? I'd come up with this idea several years earlier. My Colombian buddy, Edgar Palacios from Philadelphia, and I had met the first day of the professional coach certification program at Pittsburgh's Duquesne University. Edgar drove across the state once a month for the weekend classes. We hit it off right away, and at the end of the first weekend, I invited him to stay at my house the next month. He did so month after month, and we became fast friends. We talked about literally everything: our shared Christian faith, sports, family, and, of course, our coaching classes.

About halfway through the program, one of our Friday dinner-conversation topics started off with me lamenting that I wasn't making any real progress in learning Spanish. I'd wanted to be fluent in Spanish for years. I thought it might be from God and would certainly be helpful in my work. Edgar, who, as I said, is originally from Colombia, loved the idea and jumped on the theme that total immersion is the only answer. In his slightly accented, perfect English, he said I needed to go live in either Colombia or Costa Rica, because they speak the best Spanish, in his opinion. I should go for at least six months, but preferably for a year. My first reaction was, "That's impossible! I can't leave my life for that long!" We kicked it around for a bit longer, then drifted off to other topics.

The next morning, I woke up and wanted to throw something at Edgar – hard. Before I even opened my eyes, I realized that my subconscious mind (or was it the Lord?) had been hard at work, because I had a fully-formed plan for immersion Spanish learning. I could become an itinerant handyman and life coach to missionaries in South America! I figured I could contact various missionaries through my church, stay with them for a while, make some repairs, help some people, speak more and more Spanish, and then move on to the next place. After all, who didn't need things to be fixed for free? Who wouldn't want free coaching?

I got all excited about this for a while, but it never developed any traction other than an interested nod of the head and an "Uh huh" comment from whoever I was talking with. Over time, I almost forgot about it, but never quite completely. Just in case, I had continued to pick away at my expensive Spanish Rosetta Stone program and the phrase CDs I'd gotten from the library. Nothing had come from that grand vision years earlier, but what about now?

Go *Where?*

Moving to South America to learn Spanish didn't seem like it was the answer to this vague prompting to "Go." The sense continued through the spring with no new revelation and I began to wonder whether I was imagining it. But I knew that wasn't the case. The sense of something coming was as strong as ever, and I resolved to continue to stay the course. Summer came and went.

Fast forward to a breakfast in early October. My good friend and pastor, Blaine Workman, and I were scheduled for one of our regular early Friday morning breakfasts. Blaine and I had become friends when our now-grown kids were in elementary school together twenty years earlier. He was one of the people I'd gone to for advice regarding this "Go" sense, but we really hadn't discussed it in much detail. It was to be the main topic of breakfast discussion that particular Friday.

After we ordered our food, Blaine said he hadn't intended to make any firm suggestions, but was feeling compelled to make a specific recommendation that he felt was from the Lord. I sensed something was going to happen – finally a breakthrough. He then asked me if I'd ever considered serving at Bongolo Hospital. The air went out of my balloon. I knew enough to know that my church had supported this rural jungle hospital for more than 30 years, but I was shocked Blaine would suggest there, of all places.

"No" was my totally serious and instantaneous reply. He looked surprised, so I expanded. "It's in Africa!" I figured that was all I'd need to say, but instead of commiserating, he looked confused. So I continued and described how I'm an urban bachelor, enjoy all four seasons, can't stand heat and high humidity, and don't want to be anywhere near malaria or AIDS epidemics, let alone Ebola! I've had plenty of friends go on short-term trips to Kenya, and my best friend growing up had been a missionary in both South Africa and Mozambique for years. I was happy to pray for and to financially support them, but I'd never had even the slightest desire to visit Africa for *any* reason.

I'd known about Bongolo Hospital pretty much since I began attending ACAC in the early 1990's. My church has been a major supporter since the Hospital's inception in 1977. In fact, we were the sending church for Dr. David Thompson, the missionary surgeon called to start the hospital. He and his replacement, Dr. Keir Thelander, had spoken at our church several times. I'd enjoyed their stories of faith in the jungle in the face of opposition and hardships, but I had never been *remotely* interested in going there.

To better paint the picture, Bongolo is located in the southeastern corner of the country of Gabon. Gabon, a former French colony, is on the western coast of Central Africa, directly below the "hump." The equator almost perfectly divides the country north and south. Think of Tarzan's birthplace and you'll be in the right neighborhood, literally. There are very few people, and lots of jungle.

The northern half of Gabon had long been exposed to the life-transforming gospel of Jesus Christ, but the southern half was completely unreached until the 1930s when the first Christian and Missionary Alliance (C&MA) missionaries, Donald Fairley and his team, arrived at the base of Bongolo Falls. They purchased land all around the Falls and, on the three plateaus above the Falls, built homes and established a church and schools, which thrived for decades. In 1977, the hospital portion opened on the lowest plateau when David Thompson and a handful of nurses arrived. Today, it is a sprawling complex with 158 beds. They provide all aspects of Western medical care to more than 40,000 patients a year.

Their surgeons annually perform approximately 2,200 procedures of all types, 450 of which are eye operations.

Additionally, Bongolo has become internationally known as a faith-based teaching hospital that trains up the equivalent of U.S. board-certified missionary surgeons as well as qualified nurses for future service in Africa. Most significantly, more than 2,200 patients a year profess new faith in Christ! So yes, I knew a little bit about Bongolo Hospital.

But Blaine couldn't be put off that easily, and asked me to hear him out. He went on to describe how Paul Davis, Bongolo's maintenance director, has had serious medical problems. He had, for the second time in two or three years, been hospitalized in America. He was back at Bongolo, but needed a vacation in addition to all kinds of help. He has a team of laborers and repairmen, but there was way more repair work and projects around the missionaries' homes and the Hospital than he or his team could handle. Blaine also told me that the missionary team could greatly benefit from coaching and my entrepreneurial background.

In that instant, my world stood stock still. *Missionaries needing handyman work and coaching?* That sounded just like my hare-brained plan to learn Spanish, a plan I'd never shared with Blaine, by the way. I had a feeling I had my answer to "Go," but I made a last ditch attempt to avoid the obvious. "I don't suppose they speak Spanish there, do they?" I asked. "No," Blaine replied, "they speak French." Drat! But by then, the hook had been firmly set. Blaine had unknowingly tapped into a dormant dream. Until that moment, however, I had not considered how selfish the Spanish idea was. I suddenly realized that I had wanted to be fluent primarily for my benefit and purposes. Serving God with that skill was secondary. I felt horrible.

The difference then and there was that I knew what Blaine was suggesting was from God rather than of "me." I also knew in my heart that my search was over. I had my answer; I was going to Africa. Nearly instantaneously, the whisper to "Go" transformed into a command: "*Go!*" I felt freed up inside as I made myself available for God's will to unfold in my life. My sense of possible calling had become a mandate.

"Okay, I'll go" was my repy a few seconds later. I could tell Blaine thought I was reacting emotionally, because he told me I needed to pray about it over the next week or so before making a decision. I remember looking at him and telling him I would do so, but that I was going.

Right after that, I found myself praying silently, "God, if this is of You, throw open all of the doors. It's Your trip. If this isn't Your idea, slam them all shut, because I'm head-strong enough to try to go on my own." I knew, however, that this calling was from God because it was nothing I ever would have come up with on my own. In fact, it was the opposite of any of my ideas, but it felt exactly right. What's more, He quickly began to answer my prayer to open the doors beyond my ability to fathom.

Why Me?

Before moving on with the story, we need to pause to reflect on the seismic change that had just happened in my life. *Me?* Why would God call me, of all people, to go to a place like Bongolo Hospital? It was mind boggling, to be honest. Many people may push back when we consider our unworthiness of being used by God in a new and different way. We may tend to think that to be utilized by God, we need to be a superstar athlete or entertainer, or a business mogul, or a recovered addict or redeemed murderer, or supremely educated and gifted like the Apostle Paul. I know I have certainly struggled with this idea of service and my "normalcy."

After all, I'm just me, an average American middle-class guy, who works hard to make ends meet, and hopefully build a future from which others can benefit. I'm nobody special as far as the world is concerned. I'm not a seminary-trained pastor, and certainly not a doctor, nurse, or any other kind of medical professional. I'm also not wealthy or a professional athlete. I sing well enough for karaoke, but nobody would ever pay me to perform, much less attend to hear me. I'm not even married with great relationships with my wife and kids. I'm just a regular guy who's gone through his share of good and bad life experiences.

I am nothing special age-wise, either. At the time of this writing, I am 53 years old. Even though that's pretty old to younger folks, my progressing age doesn't really matter much to me. I've noticed that being called "sir" doesn't bother me anymore. In fact, now it sounds more like a respectful tip-of-the-hat, rather than something age-related. In fact, most days I feel like I'm years younger than my age. I stay fit and follow a healthy regimen without going off the deep end in any particular category, and have learned to focus on getting enough sleep.

In fact, I'm proud to say I still fit into the tuxedo I bought 15 years ago, even though I think I've stretched out the waist of my trousers a little bit. I've found, however, that I must eat and drink far less than I used to in order to keep it this way.

Just recently, I came face-to-face with a new idea regarding my age, and that's how I am perceived by somebody a generation younger than I am. While I was at Bongolo Hospital, Dr. Elizabeth (Izzi) Elliott, an early-30s surgeon, was telling a story at a group dinner and made the comment that I'd been an adult for as long as she's been alive! Based on the context of the story, I decided that she intended it as a compliment because when I gave her a funny look, her animated expression didn't budge a bit and she didn't stop talking. It doesn't change the reality that to many people, I'm older.

I'm also nobody special when it comes to money and career success. Don't get me wrong, I've done okay. I've been self-employed since 2002 and before that, I had a successful career as a corporate sales executive. Amazingly, I've now been an entrepreneur for longer than I was an employee. Throughout the years, I've changed directions several times, and like many, I've ridden the financial roller coaster. I've had to recover from losing half of everything in a divorce only to stare at a possible bankruptcy years later when the economy tanked. I'd had great jobs and won awards, but I've also been laid off. I've dealt with bad credit, debt collectors, and prayed over which bills I'd pay this month. Things financially have been much more stable these last few years, and I've really come to appreciate that. Like many, I've struggled with the question of whether or not I balanced living up to my economic potential in light of what else God wanted me to spend my time on.

The world also says that I'm nobody special when it comes to my personal life. While many of my friends are celebrating their 25th and 30th wedding anniversaries, I've been divorced since 2001 and have not remarried. I've been blessed by a couple of longer dating relationships, but they ended when one of us felt it wouldn't work out in the long run. While my friends celebrate graduations, plan weddings, and brag about their grandchildren, I'm in the second decade of a depth of pain I wouldn't wish on anyone. I'm still estranged from my grown children who, because of the divorce, still don't want anything to do with me or their grandparents (my parents).

I'm not anything special at church either. Compared to those fortunate to become a Christian in their early years, I'm a later-in-life convert. I lived a lot of life before surrendering myself to God and His ways twenty-five years ago. I've been a member of the same church since the early 1990s and, like many of us, have been involved in a lot of ministries. I played my violin as part of the worship orchestra, taught fourth and fifth graders for several years, helped out in senior high classes, been a leader in the men's ministry, and led different small groups for years. I've never been an elder, deacon, or trustee, and I've never really wanted to serve that way, to be honest with you.

Nope. I'm nothing special as far as the world is concerned, and that's exactly the kind of person God loves to get His hands on!

God Calls Gideon and Samuel

It's a good thing the Bible is chock full of characters who could also be seen as "totally average" up until a certain point in their lives. I need to re-read these great stories every once in a while to remind me just how human our heroes were. One of my favorite "calling" accounts is when God enlisted Gideon, perhaps the most "normal" of any hero of Scripture.

I could always relate to Gideon. He was hiding from the enemy and preparing food in light of the imminent invasion of the Midianites. He was just a normal guy doing what he had to do to survive. Suddenly, an angel appeared and had the following conversation with scared, trembling Gideon:

> Then the angel of the Lord came and sat beneath the great tree at Ophrah, which belonged to Joash of the clan of Abiezer. Gideon son of Joash was threshing wheat at the bottom of a winepress to hide the grain from the Midianites. The angel of the Lord appeared to him and said, *"Mighty hero, the Lord is with you!"*
>
> "Sir," Gideon replied, "if the Lord is with us, why has all this happened to us? And where are all the miracles our ancestors told us about? Didn't they say, 'The Lord brought us up out of Egypt'? But now the Lord has abandoned us and handed us over to the Midianites." Then the Lord turned to him and said, *"Go with the strength you have, and rescue Israel from the Midianites. I am sending you!"*
>
> "But Lord," Gideon replied, "how can I rescue Israel? My clan is the weakest in the whole tribe of Manasseh, and I am the least in my entire family!" The Lord said to him, *"I will be with you.*

And you will destroy the Midianites as if you were fighting against one man." (Judges 6:11-17 NLT emphasis added).

God called Gideon a mighty warrior before Gideon even realized God wanted him to be a soldier. Then, after Gideon objected, God told Gideon to go with whatever strength he currently possessed. The key for Gideon was to obey and to get going. "I am sending you" was our Creator saying He knew what He was doing and would provide everything Gideon needed because going was His idea. This command made absolutely no sense to the frustrated and somewhat flummoxed Gideon, so he objected again. God's reply was, "I will be with you," and He ensured Gideon's victory. In the verses that follow, God even patiently permitted Gideon to go through the well-known "fleece" process to prove that this message was truly from God. It had a deep impact on me when I realized that God planned for Gideon to be successful *before* Gideon ever agreed to go. Gideon's mission was God's idea, and that was all Gideon needed to know.

Another biblical call I have also resonated with, mostly because of regret for my rebellious years, is when God first contacted Samuel while he was still a young boy. One night, God called to Samuel three times. After the first two instances, Samuel ran each time to his teacher Eli's bed, eager to help and trying to respond as best he could. By then, Eli realized that it was God who was calling to Samuel, so Eli gave Samuel instructions to answer the voice when it called again. God called a third time and Samuel obeyed. I wish I had learned to listen for and respond to God at such a young age.

Frankly, it seems that everybody God utilizes either quickly or eventually makes the decision to become available and to do things God's way. Gideon did, so did Samuel. Fortunately, God didn't give up on me, no matter how many times I messed up. I finally got to the point where, regardless of my life circumstances, I had decided my role was to always answer, "Here I am, Lord. I'm available for whatever You want," even if that meant going to the jungles of Africa.

Why *not* Me?

Therefore, perhaps, a better question than "Why me?" would be, "Why *not* me?" What if I actually have a specialized role in helping to fulfill God's purpose? What if my completely normal life, complete with good and bad times, and a unique set of skills, strengths, weaknesses, and experiences was exactly what God wants to utilize to accomplish His specific objectives? *What if I'm exactly the right person to complete a mission on God's behalf?*

I have come to the conclusion that this is true. God loves me far more than I can ever comprehend and, in spite of what I might think or feel, His opinion counts for a whole lot more than mine or that of anyone else, for that matter. Among many, many Scriptures that support this, one of my favorites was written by Paul, a fellow later-in-life convert to Christianity, who, before he met Jesus, did a lot more terrible things than I ever will:

> And I am convinced that *nothing* can ever sep-
> arate us from God's love. *Neither* death nor life,
> neither angels nor demons, neither our fears for
> today nor our worries about tomorrow—not even
> the powers of hell can separate us from God's
> love. *No power* in the sky above or in the earth
> below—indeed, *nothing* in all creation will ever be
> able to separate us from the love of God that is
> revealed in Christ Jesus our Lord (Romans 8:38-39
> NLT emphasis added).

The truth in that passage has taken a long time to really sink in. I've dropped the ball many times, and sometimes it feels like I've failed more than I've succeeded. Can you relate to that feeling? Yet, if God can save and fully utilize a man like Paul,

He can certainly use you and me — if we will let Him do so. What if all I have to do is listen, surrender, and trust?

Because of fear, however, it's easy to pull back from serving to our full capacity. My good friend and mentor, John Stanko, loves to make people think while they laugh at his humor, and he teaches on this issue of fear, prayer, and obeying God. Every time he paints the picture of how fear tends to limit my permission for God to use me, it's a fresh reminder for me to be strong.

John starts by holding out both arms as far to each side as he can, in a position of submission, prayer, and supplication. He then cries out in prayer, "God, I'll do anything for you!" He pauses for effect, then starts a funny and sad downward progression: "I'll do anything you want as long as it's not in Africa (or some other country)!" As he says this, both of his arms come just a little bit toward the middle. "As long as it's not outside of the United States!" and his arms and hands get a little closer together. "As long as it's in my city!" His hands are now much closer together. "As long as it's at my church!" He concludes this with, "As long as it's at my church on Sunday between 9:00 and 11:00 in the morning!"

By this time, there's just the tiniest gap between his hands. His audience's laughter gets more and more subdued as John drives his point home: Go when and where God calls you, and do it now. No negotiating. Now. John isn't saying don't serve your church. That's not his point, so don't let that distract you. John's point is that many people so narrowly limit God's calling on their lives that it all but disappears, and consequently they miss out on the blessings God has in mind for them.

When I sat there in the restaurant with Blaine Workman, I felt this self-limiting progression begin inside of me as soon as he suggested going to Bongolo. *Africa? The deep jungle?*

Heat and humidity? Bugs? Malaria? AIDS? Ebola? French? No restaurants? I'm the ultimate urban bachelor for goodness sake! It would have been all too easy to decide this idea wasn't for me. I mean, nearly every prayer about missions work I've ever prayed always seems to end with, ". . . as long as it's not in the jungles of Africa."

Fortunately, John's teaching flashed through my mind while I sat there with Blaine. I also remember thinking, "No, darn it! This time, I'm not going to limit God. I've told Him I'm available. I've slowly learned to trust Him for what's best in my life and have experienced the benefits of surrendering to His will for me. This time, I'm going to put that trust to work at a whole new level. I *am* available. Use me. Send me, if that's what You want."

And that's exactly what He did.

From Over Here to Over There

After I made myself 100% available to God's call to Bongolo, I also chose to give Him control of the process. I wanted to emulate Gideon in this. Saying that and then doing so, however, was no easy task for me. I'm an independent, take-charge entrepreneur, and have been this way my whole life. It's been especially true since leaving the corporate world to work for myself. There are two things most people don't think about when they consider having their own company. The first is often described in the form of an old joke. The setup line is that when you work for yourself you get to work half days! The punch line is that we get to choose which twelve hours! The other thing that employees don't tend to think about is that if a small business owner doesn't produce results, then there's no money for food or any other expenses. Therefore, those of us who run our own companies tend to be independent, "get things done" people, otherwise we don't eat.

I wanted my going to Bongolo Hospital to happen only if God wanted it to. I knew in my own strength that I could have set up my own trip. After all, how hard could it be to buy plane tickets, get a visa and shots, and head over? I could have coordinated all of this with somebody at the Hospital and been on my way. That's not the point in question. The thing I needed to definitively know was whether or not God wanted me to go on this trip in the first place.

As agreed, Blaine and I got back together two weeks later. He again painted the picture of what he thought I might do there, and asked me if I still thought I was being called to go to Bongolo. "Yes, absolutely" was my immediate answer. However, a complicating factor emerged while we talked: I had the overwhelming sense that God wanted me to go pretty quickly. Blaine had suggested going the following summer, but that felt all wrong. He then threw out going in January (keep in mind this was the middle of October!). That felt just right. When Blaine said I might go for a couple of weeks, however, that felt wrong, again. He had described a pretty large mission that could barely even begin in two weeks. So I immediately countered that I thought I would need to stay for at least a month, and Blaine's eyes got big. By the end of breakfast, we'd settled on two months, leaving in January. That meant there were only three months to plan, fundraise, break the news to my parents, find a house-sitter, get mandatory immunization shots, organize my home and work life, and everything else that would need to happen. "God, open all of these doors or slam them shut!" was my constant prayer. From that point forward, He started blasting open doors I didn't even know existed.

A few times when I didn't think things were happening fast enough, I felt myself trying to take over the process. At those times, it was as if God gently slapped my grasping hand in rebuke. "Oh, yeah," I would mumble, "Sorry!" Over and over, I had to confess my impatience and distrust. "Yes, we agreed this was *Your* trip and that I would help only when You want me to. The rest of the time, I promised that I would sit quietly and watch. That way I could experience Your love and power in a new way. I'm sorry!" Every time I backed down, something marvelous happened, sometimes nearly right away.

One of these "grasping" times had to do with my nervousness about getting all of my immunization shots done on time, and especially the yellow fever vaccination. Without this particular shot, I would not be allowed into Gabon, or almost anywhere else in Africa, for that matter. I learned that my local Health Department administered travel vaccinations as well as local private express doctor offices, but the latter were a lot more expensive. Therefore, I called the Health Department and got a very nice lady on the phone. She told me that yellow fever was in short supply and that currently there was none in Western Pennsylvania! She said they should get more before I wanted to travel, but she also advised that I begin searching regionally. I reported this back to Barb Lanser who, with her husband, Rod, were also going. This was their third trip to Bongolo, and I relied heavily on Barb's experience regarding travel details.

That same day, I started researching other vaccination options. I went so far as to look up the Health Department in Buffalo, NY, close to my parents' home in Hamburg. Then I remembered my promise to God: this is *His* trip and I'm to help only when He tells me to. "I'm sorry again!" I took a deep breath and handed control of my vaccinations over to Him, where they were supposed to be in the first place. When I did, His peace descended on me and I literally forgot about it.

Early the next morning, Barb texted me, instructing me to drop everything and make an appointment at one of the private express doctor offices near my home – they had the yellow fever vaccination, but it was in short supply. I did so, and got an appointment for a few days later. Not only was this way sooner than I thought possible, it was a better answer than I would have come up with, because it turned out that my health insurance covered most of the shots!

I marveled as I observed this pattern repeat itself over and over again before leaving for Gabon. It quickly became clear that God really did want me to go to Bongolo, and He blew open every single door to demonstrate this to me! He handled house-sitting, caring for Tutu (my cat), fundraising, bill paying while gone, how to slow down my businesses so I could leave with confidence my clients would wait for me, itinerary and airplane tickets, the church's administrative process, my Gabonese visa (a great story in its own right), what to take, how to pack, and on and on.

As time went on, it got easier to let go of my desire to

control the process. It's amazing how relaxed and contented I was when I did so! By the time I headed for the airport on January 21, 2016, I knew I was following God's plan for me. Like Gideon, I was going in the strength I had. I was filled with trust that God would bring His plan to fruition in ways I couldn't even begin to imagine. I had not felt this kind of excitement in years. People repeatedly asked me if I was nervous. My reply was always the same: "No, not at all. In fact, I'm really confident! Either I'm not smart enough to be scared, or I'm experiencing God's perfect peace."

I was confident that I had God's peace and I intended to live in it for the entire time I was in Bongolo.

The Rest of This Book

The rest of the book consists of the actual day-to-day blogs I published while at Bongolo Hospital; I believe they capture the moments the Lord wanted me to write about and share. Each entry went out to a couple thousand people via my email distribution list, Facebook and LinkedIn. One entry makes me cry every time I tell the story; others make me laugh! Some discuss the challenges and amazing differences between a First World lifestyle and life in the jungle. Sometimes, the name of God doesn't appear at all, but don't worry about that! You can be assured that He was and is at the heart of everything I wrote.

It didn't seem to be enough to simply journal about stories or to convey information. And honestly speaking, how many people would want to read a personal journal? God desired me to grow from my experiences, so at the end of each entry, there is a "Lessons Learned" section where I reflect on my takeaways. This is followed by a related question to ponder as it relates to where you and I are in our lives. Finally, each day concludes with an affirmation of possibility.

I pray these entries uplift you, that you will have your prayers answered regarding God's call on your life, and that they will inspire and equip you to step out and do what God has put in your heart to do.

An Overview

I wrote my first entry on the airplane somewhere over the Atlantic Ocean between JFK Airport in New York City and Paris, France, the mid-point of my journey to Gabon. I don't know how I managed to do so, as I was physically crushed between the man next to me and the window. Here it is:

Wow, is it a lot of work to rush the preparation to go on a last minute two-month trip, especially when the prep work spanned the Thanksgiving and Christmas holidays! Fortunately, I've always been a list maker, so it was no surprise that I had several to-do lists going at any given time in an effort to keep things straight. Here are some of the category headings I used: packing, shopping, gifts, friend meetings, work arrangements, notes regarding hospital personnel, trip objectives, personal objectives, and so on. As my departure approached, these lists seemed to grow and grow instead of getting shorter. Somehow I managed to get the most important things done. More importantly, I got to spend precious time with family and dear friends. There wasn't much sleep the final week, but I considered that a price well worth paying.

As a recap, this is my first ever mission trip. While I've always wanted to go on a short-term trip through church, that hadn't happened. God, in His perfect timing, wanted me on this one. I'm traveling with four others from Pittsburgh: Ray and Barb Lanser, our leaders for their two weeks at Bongolo; Ray Wolfgang, a retired engineer who loves going on mission trips; and Bobby Shriver, a mid-30s framing contractor who's gone on two other mission trips. So I'm the rookie, and I'm really grateful to be part of this team, even though they will only be there for two of my eight weeks.

I'm going to be living and working at Bongolo Hospital,

located in the jungle of southeastern Gabon, Africa. While there, I will be filling in for Paul Davis, the maintenance director, while he takes some long overdue vacation. I will be supervising his crew of eight Gabonese men, as well as work on whatever projects and repairs he has on his agenda. I have also been asked by my church leaders to explore longer-term goals with hospital leadership, staff and community leaders to answer the question: How can ACAC more meaningfully participate with Bongolo Hospital? Additionally, I will be a player-coach for the first phase of building a new eye surgery center, a projected two-year project. God only knows what else I'll be doing!

Amazingly, I raised more support money for the trip than I thought was possible in a short period of time, and I'm grateful to the friends and family who gave on my behalf. Humanly speaking, raising this amount during Christmas and New Year's seemed to be impossible, but I kept reminding myself that this is God's trip. All monies were collected and transparently administered by my church. Friends, family and church friends donated online and dropped checks in the offering plate during worship services. Amazingly, the entire amount needed for me to peacefully step away from my Pittsburgh life for two months was covered prior to my departure.

This is clearly God's trip, and my prayer is that I continue to surrender to Him and trust the fact that He knows best. He has made this trip possible and I'm excited and full of anticipation of serving Him at Bongolo.

Lessons Learned So Far

1. Plan, but be extremely flexible.
2. Pray, and keep remembering that God is in charge and I'm not.

3. Calm and patience are a better way to live than stress, frustration and impatience.

To Ponder

How can I apply these lessons to my life today?

Affirmation

I am flexible and creative!

Adrenaline and Exhaustion

For years, my friends told me their stories of international travel to Asia, India, Australia, and South America — tales of grueling, 24-plus hours of travel, endless airplane flights, and jetlag. I couldn't relate to their experiences, until today.

I'm writing this early Saturday morning in Libreville, Gabon, three quarters of the way to Bongolo Hospital. We left my home in Pittsburgh at 9:30 AM on Thursday, for Pittsburgh International Airport. Our first flight was to JFK Airport in New York City. After a planned five-hour layover, we departed on a flight for Paris. That 6.5-hour flight was smooth and on time, but I'll never again ask for a window exit row seat. There was even less room than a normal economy class seat because the exit door juts out and takes away much-needed leg room!

Two and a half hours after touching down in Paris, we took off on another seven-hour flight, this time bound for Libreville, the capitol of Gabon. Libreville is located on the Atlantic Ocean in the northwest corner of the country. Upon our arrival, we were glad to be met at the airport by Pastor Sangoye who works for Bongolo Hospital. Even better news was that all of our luggage arrived, including the crates we brought with us with supplies for the missionaries. From there, we went for a late dinner with Rob Peterson, Bongolo's pilot, then spent the night at the Hospital's guest house. It was incredibly hot, but it was the best sleep I'd had in days. My adrenaline has been so high that I've not been able to totally relax. I have barely slept a total of six hours the last three nights, yet have felt remarkably good.

Lessons Learned So Far

1. **Expectation management is critical.** Fortunately, I came

mentally prepared to sit on a plane or in an airport for the better part of two days. Even though exhausted, I didn't sleep much, so I had the challenge of finding ways to pass long hours.

2. **Systems get developed enroute.** I got better at managing the security checkpoints at each of our various stops. What is the fastest way to load my carry-on bags, laptops (mine and a donated one), shoes, reading glasses, and other personal items? How do I handle passport and ticket organization and presentation? Do I talk with the airport security people? (Yes, of course. All of them were very nice and seemed to appreciate being treated like people.)

3. **Learning a little French has been well-received.** I had my first complete dialogue in French with a flight attendant offering me a snack and a drink. He was the first person not to address me in English. The French words I used really worked!

4. **Friendship and faith cross language barriers.** The Frenchman (Jeff) who sat next to me on the Paris flight slept most of the time, but it turned out he spoke adequate English. As we approached Paris, we finally spoke, and I learned that he and his wife had just been on a mission trip to Brazil to work with drug addicts!

To Ponder

How can I apply travel lessons to my life today?

Affirmation

Handling new situations on the fly is easy for me!

Arrival at Bongolo Hospital

Early Saturday morning, we flew the final leg of our trip in a small, five-seat Cessna airplane. Bongolo's missionary pilot, Rob Peterson, makes one or two runs every week from Libreville to Bongolo's landing field (about 350 miles) just outside of Lébamba, the small town 15 minutes from the hospital. What a great experience! Much of the time, we were below the clouds and we had great views. Gabon is about the size of Pennsylvania and New York combined, yet only has a population of about 1.6 million people. Almost 800,000 live in Libreville, while another 300,000 live in the next seven largest cities. That leaves just 500,000 people spread throughout the rest of the country. There are a few towns of less than 20,000 people; the vast majority of the rest live in hundreds and hundreds of small villages tucked into the jungle and connected by mostly red dirt roads.

Upon landing at 11:30 AM, we drove 15 minutes from the dirt air strip through Lébamba, the largest nearby town of about 4,500 people, and saw primitive lifestyles the likes of which I had tried to imagine, but I wasn't ready for how the scenes would emotionally impact me — literally to tears. There were small one- or two-room shacks that I automatically assumed were abandoned and condemned, but they were everywhere and housed large families. There was inadequate electricity, no indoor plumbing, windows without glass or even screens, and dirt or concrete floors. The people we saw, however, appeared to be well-fed and content, with children playing and people sitting outside talking.

We were warmly greeted at the residence portion of the sprawling Hospital compound, and Bobby, Ray and I (Rod and Barb Lanser are housed in another home) were shown to our rooms in the "Annex." This is a small, sterile, dorm-like portion of a three-unit residence. The quarters were clean, modern, and comfortable. Considering what we drove past, I'm grateful for what I was already thinking about as luxuries: electricity, drinkable running water, plenty of ceiling and box fans, and a comfortable bed. Even the homes at Bongolo don't have full glass windows to which Americans are accustomed. The simple explanation for this is there is no air conditioning and, of course, no need for heating. However, they all have bug screens and security bars; some have louvered glass panes that don't seem to shut all the way. While we're not quite sure yet, our best guess is to keep out the rain if it's windy.

We spent the rest of the day getting settled in and meeting some of the missionaries (and their families) and exploring. That evening (Saturday), we had dinner with Paul and Meladee Davis, the director of maintenance and his wife, who we'd be spending a lot of time with once work starts on Monday. We went "home" full and exhausted.

Lessons Learned So Far

1. Small airplanes avoid flying into clouds because they can severely damage the plane, perhaps even ripping off a wing. We went above, under, and around clouds during our journey. That provided an interesting life metaphor for me: There may be really good reasons to take what seems to be the painfully slow, round-about way rather than blast straight ahead.

2. One man's condemned building is another man's castle. When in a new culture, ask questions and check pride and judgmental assumptions at the door.

3. It's easy at first to complain when something isn't the way I want it to be. I was really hoping for more of a "homey" living space than what we were given, which is a dorm environment with no real kitchen or living room spaces.

However, seeing the primitive living conditions on the way from the air strip effectively stopped my grumbling in its tracks!

To Ponder

How would I respond to living in abject, primitive poverty for an extended period of time?

Affirmation

Gratitude for what I have is a natural part of me!

The biblical concept of Sabbath rest is observed on the Hospital campus, except for necessary medical staffing. Otherwise, it's a day off. In spite of jetlag, we attended the large open air church on the Hospital grounds. Built in the 1930s by the first missionaries, it is a gigantic one-room rectangle capable of seating 1,000 people. The sides are open "windows" with no glass. The peak of the steeply vaulted roof line rises 30 feet above our heads. In the future, I'd like to attend the small village C&MA churches, but today it is the main church.

About 600 or so adults and half as many children were packed into the thin, insect-eaten wooden benches. All were locals except for some of the missionaries who attend there. Church often lasts more than three hours and we were invited to check out the Sunday school area part way through the service. This was a double blessing, since it was quite hot and the singing and preaching were in French with no translation. It was easy to see, however, that it was a Spirit-filled venue!

Afterwards, while walking back from church up steep "Cardiac Hill" to the Station where the missionaries live, I saw my first snake! We were halfway down the back road that loops around the Hospital when we stopped to admire a beautiful 150-foot-tall tree. Ignoring my friends' calls not to go into the tall grass, I walked to get a closer look at the trunk when I caught a quick glimpse of a startled two or three foot long, bright green snake. To my friend's laughter, I traveled the ten feet back to the road faster than I thought I could move! That night, I looked online to see if I could discover what kind of snake it was, and all of the contenders were poisonous. I'm glad I jumped back as fast as I did! It was then that I learned all Gabonese snakes are poisonous. Of course they are.

After lunch, we drove into Lébamba to do some food

shopping for the week. Imagine a red-dirt road up to the main section of town when the road becomes concrete, with food vendors on both sides, a traffic circle, and a few small indoor stores. I didn't do any shopping, but helped by carrying bags. What an overwhelming cultural experience that was, made harder because of the language barrier. The whole thing was foreign compared to what I was accustomed, yet somehow familiar at the same time. Unfortunately, the person who took us speaks no French, so the shopping was more difficult.

For dinner, we were again hosted by another medical missionary family, Eric and Dr. Wendy Hoffman, and their three children under the age of four: Esther, Eli, and baby Hannah. Wendy is the head eye surgeon here and Eric is the Chief Financial Officer at the hospital. What a wonderful, laughter-filled evening we enjoyed. By the end, Esther and Eli were playing and talking with us like we were family! They were very good around adults they had just met.

Lessons Learned So Far

1. People on this side of the globe worship the same God we do in America, even though I couldn't understand what was being sung or said.

2. Kids in this culture are adorable, just like back home.

3. It's best to assume all Gabonese snakes are poisonous.

4. Don't be afraid to try new things — American ways aren't the only ways.

5. Ideally, go shopping with someone who can translate to prevent mistakes and being taken advantage of in a bartering environment.

To Ponder

*How can I explore new things safely,
yet with a spirit of adventure?*

Affirmation

It's so much fun to try new things!

Construction Work

We've completed our first two full days of work on the new eye clinic. This clinic is a huge building project for Bongolo, with two stories and approximately 50 feet wide by 125 feet long. It is projected to be a two-year project. The funding is from a $600,000 grant from USAID, a U.S. federal agency that funds hospital and secondary school construction projects around the world. It's an exciting opportunity, since this is the first project they've done with the Christian and Missionary Alliance, my church's (ACAC) denomination. When this goes well, they expect other projects to follow, either here or elsewhere in the world. It's also a great project because we must adhere to U.S. safety and building code standards, which is a new experience for the southern Gabonese contractor.

It was started only a month ago, and we arrived to find the metal super-structure built, the 130-plus metal ceiling joists loosely positioned, the gigantic handicap ramp up to the second floor in place and installed, and the roof partially on! The team from Ohio that's been here for the last month is at least a week ahead of schedule and our work team of four (Rod, Bobby, Ray, and myself) will be forever grateful to them because it looks like we'll get to work mostly in the shade! In this heat, that's a huge blessing.

We have been assigned two major jobs. The first is to carefully position, square up, and weld into place the second floor steel floor joists, which are about 25 feet long and must weigh at least a couple hundred pounds each. Because of the 50 foot width of the building, there is a center beam where the joists butt together. Our job is to place them at 24-inch intervals, squared to the main beams already in place, and weld them into position. Even with labor-saving pry bars, this is very physical work.

Our second project is to lay down and weld the proper size corrugated aluminum sheets (approximately three feet wide of varying lengths between 20 and 24 feet,) which will be the base of the second floor subfloor. These are also very heavy and awkward to maneuver. We had a lot of organization and gathering to do since many of them were spread all over the second floor area, being used as walking paths and scaffold platforms. The other third are still bundled and waiting to be lifted up to the second floor. For some reason, the architects designed it this way, but it didn't make a lot of sense to us. We've got our work cut out for us between these two projects.

There are two tricky parts. The first is that all our work is about 20 feet off the ground and, for now, that is just plain terrifying for me. I'll adjust, but it will take a few more days. In spite of my house remodeling experience, I've never worked a construction site like this and these two days have consisted of "keep going in spite of the fear." It took everything in me that first Monday morning to step across a three-foot gap onto the first platform. I was literally shuddering as I watched the far more experienced Rod, Bobby, and Ray walk on the four-inch joists in every possible direction as if they were at ground level. They're aware of my fear and have been great, not pushing me past my comfort zone, yet encouraging me to learn. I'm grateful to say that I've gotten more and more comfortable over time. I'm proud to say that I've also not held back the pace of work.

The second tricky thing is the heat. We were advised to drink as much as possible and all us are staying hydrated enough so as not to get heat sick. Every day, I am drinking at least six 1.5 liter bottles of water or Gatorade from powder we brought along. This might be too much information for some people, but in spite of how much I drank, I didn't pee all day long from first thing in the morning until nearly dinner time. Only before bedtime have I started to feel at all like my thirst was quenched — that's how hot it is here.

Lessons Learned So Far

1. It's okay to be scared. It's also okay to tell the right people. I'm grateful for the three guys who gave me the space to get used to working at a height on very narrow platforms.

2. Hard work makes for a clear mind and good sleeping. I've been exhausted!

3. Feeling dehydrated all day stinks. Somehow, I need to drink even more tomorrow.

To Ponder

On to what "platform" can I step out in faith today?

Affirmation

*I'm proud of myself when I overcome
something that previously scared me!*

Hospital Tour

At the end of another hot, dehydrated, yet productive day of work on the eye clinic today, we were given a 90-minute tour of the hospital. Dr. Keir Thelander (pronounced "Keer"), the medical director and missionary team leader, took time out of his day to give us some history, show us around, and describe some future expansion plans. We'd knocked off work at 3:00 so we could get cleaned up before the tour started at 4:00.

Christian missionaries have been in this location for over 70 years and evangelism is still the primary reason Bongolo exists. The hospital was founded in 1977 when the first missionary doctor, David Thompson, arrived with three nurses and a couple of support people. David's sending church was ACAC (my church home in Pittsburgh), which partially explains our leadership's deep passion for Bongolo. It's amazing what David and his team have built throughout the years from almost nothing, in the middle of the jungle far from "civilization." Today, the sprawling campus covers the three plateaus just above the river. The doctors, residents, and administrative missionaries live in houses and apartments at the top of a steep quarter-of-a-mile hill above the hospital. Dr. Thompson has since moved on to minister in Egypt, but his legacy is going strong.

When I think of a hospital, I imagine a very large, modern, multi-story American building with hundreds of staff, physicians, nurses, plenty of parking, and the latest technology. Bongolo's 158-bed hospital, however, is made up of numerous one- and two-story white and brown stucco concrete blocks with metal roofs that were built as needed. Some equipment is newer and some is quite old. Bongolo has just a handful of missionary surgeons, six African surgical residents in training, and about 65 African nurses, many also in training or graduates of its three-year nursing program. They buy medicines from Europe and, twice a year, ship in from the States most of their equipment and supplies inside forty-foot truck containers. There is little-to-no patient privacy and each doctor is a jack-of-all trades. The most rapidly growing areas at the hospital over the last few years have been ophthalmology and maternity.

I am more than a little surprised by the seemingly make-shift nature of much of the Hospital. But I need to remember that in spite of these relatively primitive conditions, this is a five-star facility for Gabon. Patients come from hundreds of miles away for care because Bongolo has a reputation for saving lives and curing diseases with a spirit of kindness and equality of care. Dr. Keir was clear that fewer people die here than "should" because of the hand of God at work. A relationship with Jesus is unashamedly presented to every patient and, in 2015, there were more than 2,000 new Christians because of the work here.

Lessons Learned So Far

1. I want to build something that will still be growing 40 years from now.

2. Providing care and help to people who otherwise would have no hope is humbling.

3. "Primitive" is a relative concept, as is the idea of "affluence."

To Ponder

Where am I looking down on someone or something that I think is primitive?

Affirmation

I build the future every day!

Weather and Climate

It's hard to believe we left Pittsburgh a week ago already! This time last week, we had just landed at JFK airport in New York City and were waiting for our flight to Paris. Every once in a while, the speed with which we traveled to two continents makes me think about how amazing modern transportation is. Not too many years ago, our two-plus day journey from Pittsburgh to Bongolo Hospital would have taken weeks if not months. While the faster travel is mostly my preference, it's also important to choose to slow down at times. I find I observe and experience many nuances of life when I do.

In a similar vein, it would be easy to miss some incredibly interesting aspects of life at Bongolo because of the huge scope and speed of this adventure. Therefore, I've been slowing down and have noticed all kinds of big and small things. Today, let me share a few climate- and weather-related ones with you:

- Let's start with the most obvious one: It's *really* hot and humid here. I know my winter climate family and friends aren't going to want to hear this, but our high today was over 100 degrees.

- We will experience highs closer to 115 degrees before I leave here.

- Fortunately, it will cool down to a humid 75 or so tonight, and I say that tongue-in-cheek!

- The warm nights are a bigger adjustment for me than the daytime heat because there is no air conditioning anywhere, except for a few select hospital areas.

- Fortunately, most rooms and hallways in the houses and apartments have ceiling fans (with no light kits). Many bathrooms and other small rooms also have ceiling-mounted fans, which I love; otherwise, it would be unbearable in an airless bathroom!

- *None* of the windows in the homes, apartments, and

Hospital buildings (except those with air conditioning) have glass like we think of. Either there is no glass at all or the windows are covered by four to five rows of louvered glass (think of large horizontal mini-blinds), but that is not the norm.

- All windows at Bongolo are covered with bug screens and have wooden or metal dowel security bars. The local African homes are not so fortunate.

- Because of the heat and our physical work, I am drinking at least eight liters of water and Gatorade each day, and I am still dehydrated until well into the evening. Thank God we've been mostly working in the roof shade of the new eye center!

- Bongolo is currently in the midst of its mini-dry season. We've been pleasantly surprised that it has rained only twice since we arrived. On both occasions, it was a brief storm at dinner time.

- Except for today (it was sunny all day), it has been overcast with partially sunny times from dawn until about 1:00 PM. Then the sun comes out for the rest of the afternoon, along with a light breeze, with stars at night.

- I'm surprised by how much I like the daytime weather!

- Orion's Belt is a constellation I recognize in our night sky this time of year. I didn't expect that.

What a different place I've come to!

Lessons Learned So Far

1. We have been commenting among our team that it feels like we're acclimating to the heat and humidity. Even though it's gotten hotter as the week has progressed, our work has gone more easily the last couple of days.

2. I have noticed I'm not sweating *constantly*. Day or night the first few days, we all had at least a perspiration sheen and, more typically, sweat running down our faces and through all of our clothing. Sweat-soaked jeans are hard to move in!

3. Bring aloe next time! This afternoon, I got sunburned after just a few minutes working in the sun — I'd cut off the sleeves of my T-shirt and suntan lotion had missed an area of my back behind my right arm pit. Fortunately, there is a patch of aloe plants behind our house.

To Ponder

When I think about my life, what would be on my list of miscellaneous observations?

Affirmation

I adapt quickly and easily to new situations and experiences!

Open Air Market in Lébamba

It's Monday, and we worked all day, but that is not today's subject. We have now been to the mostly open air market twice in the nearest large town of Lébamba. It takes 15 minutes to drive the three or so miles because the roads are unpaved, red dirt, and quite rutted. They are paved, however, in the small town center itself. Ironically, we were told the roads are actually in good condition since it's been dryer than usual this time of year. Part of the drive to Lébamba is to go through a permanent police checkpoint. Both times, the local police did not us stop us; they simply waved us through. We were told that's because of the Bongolo Hospital signs on our SUV. The reason for these checkpoints is that there are not enough police vehicles to do American-style patrols, so they set up checkpoints instead. We are supposed to have our passports when we leave the Station/Hospital, but none of us carry them. We're trusting in the Hospital's reputation and God's favor.

Lébamba has a population of about 4,500 people. That makes it about the size of the village of Hamburg, NY, where I grew up riding my bicycle everywhere my parents didn't drive me. The difference is Hamburg is a small suburb of Buffalo, in a region of western New York State of over one million people. There are only 1.6 million people in all of Gabon, and well over half of them live in the capital city of Libreville, about a 10-hour drive north and west of here. That makes Lébamba the center of life in these parts. There are numerous tiny native villages surrounding it, all nestled in the jungle.

Most Americans would consider Lébamba slightly above primitive and the close-by villages next up for bulldozing and starting over. There is only one building over two-stories high, and not many two-story structures. Most buildings and homes are built with locally-made stone blocks and variegated steel sheet roofs. The women we saw were usually colorfully dressed in native garb; the men and kids dressed "Western." Most speak French and the local tribal language, Nzebi. I don't believe there are white residents here except for the missionaries.

Next time, I'll go more into the amazing actual shopping experience.

Lessons Learned So Far

1. Normal is relative. I've learned that there are several explanations for why people here live the way they do. I can't say I totally understand let alone agree with those reasons, but their reality is the reality around here.

2. It's good to feel shocked and offended. On our first trip to Lébamba, I was deeply shocked by the primitive living conditions. Most people have dirt floors, no running water, and limited electricity. Very few windows have screens, let alone glass louvers. It's sad, judging by Western standards.

3. It's amazing how quickly we can adapt to a new "normal." By the second trip into town (and we'd also done some other local driving), the primitive conditions didn't affect me quite as deeply. I'm still sifting through why that is.

4. Being known and respected are valuable. Bongolo Hospital magnet signs on our vehicles get us through the police checkpoints with nothing more than a friendly wave from the officers (at least this month).

To Ponder

*What nearby town or area can I explore
to expand my sense of reality?*

Affirmation

I am open-minded regarding how others live!

Open Air Market (continued)

It's Tuesday, and again we worked outside all day at the new eye center. Instead of discussing that, I want to return to our two open-air market shopping experiences. Last time, I described the physical nature of what we saw in Lébamba, the largest nearby town. Today, let's look at the actual shopping experience and differences between the first and second trips.

The first trip. For our first trip to Lébamba a week ago, we were taken to town by a kind woman from the mission who, unfortunately, does not speak French or the local tribal language, only English. Therefore, we were limited in our interaction with the market vendors. Our first stop was the local tailor. Ray, one of our team members, wanted to have a shirt and placemats made from fabric the hospital generously gives to all visitors. The tailor that many of the missionaries prefer to use lives and works on a small side street in a bright blue building that looked a lot like a single-wide trailer made of concrete with a standard corrugated metal roof. Unfortunately, he wasn't there, and his wife speaks no English. Our escort tried to communicate, but it was pointless. We'll return another day.

The shopping in Lébamba is a combination of open air stalls along one side and behind the main street, along with several small food, hardware, clothing, tire repair, and other such stores. I found the heat to be stifling, as no shops have air conditioning. It was sunny and in the 90s, and the sun felt like it was melting me through my hat and 50 SPF sunblock. I was somewhat intimidated both by not being able to communicate with anyone and not knowing whether the prices were fair.

The exchange rate calculation (about 600 Central African francs to one U.S. dollar) was too much to mentally calculate that first day. Imagine paying 1,000 francs for some fruit! That's only about $1.60, but it seemed like much more.

We also had to determine whether or not everything was a fair price. It was cheap by U.S. standards, but what about Gabonese standards? Did they increase the prices because we were white?

We managed to purchase some fruit from the street vendors and canned goods from one of the small food stores. The missionaries call the largest of the food stores their "Walmart," but that's got to be tongue in cheek because it was a little place the size of an American 7-11 convenience store that only sold frozen meat, canned food items, cheap plastic goods, juice, Coca Cola and alcohol. And it is easily the largest of Lébamba's food stores. As we headed back home, I was more than a little relieved to leave.

The second trip. Our second trip a week later was easier for several reasons. First, I was more acclimated to the heat; second, I knew what to expect in town; third, we had two fluent French speakers with us to communicate with the merchants, as well as teach us some local customs. One interesting custom relates to the street vendors: "You touch it, you buy it," unless it's bananas or something else that needs to be inspected prior to purchasing. The merchants can get agitated and animated if you violate that policy. It was amazing how much easier and safer I felt simply because of language and cultural translation.

Now I'm looking forward to shopping next time. I want to get a shirt made, buy food for meals, and secure my very own machete!

Lessons Learned So Far

1. If you don't speak the language, be with someone who does, especially if you're shopping.

2. Shopping is slow here — or, maybe that's true everywhere.

3. There is a little haggling, but not much. It doesn't appear to be a norm here. However, I can't shake the thought that

we were taken advantage of that first trip to town!

To Ponder

How can I make shopping an adventure?

Affirmation

Exploring a new culture is fun!

Teamwork

It's Wednesday night and three of our five-member team left for Pittsburgh this morning. Ray leaves in a week since we're so remote that there is no available transportation up to Libreville for several days. I'm going to miss them a lot. We laughed that such an eclectic group could bond so quickly and work so well together, especially in a foreign country and in this heat. Not once did we snap at each other in anger, frustration, or exhaustion. In fact, the heat and alien feel of Bongolo brought us together. We looked out for each other on the job site, shared countless bottles of water or Gatorade (from powder), and laughed a lot. A favorite was when Bobby heard Ray respond to, "Are you ready?" with "Goat Head," which made absolutely no sense. Ray had actually said, "Go ahead." So Bobby answered, "OK, monkey lips." Goat head and monkey lips became running jokes the rest of the week.

It also seemed we could always turn accidents into good-natured humor. For example, Rod, our grand master of construction and everything mechanical, kept us endlessly entertained by repeatedly shocking himself with a welding machine. Somehow, Bobby (who Rod trained to weld) didn't get shocked more than once or twice. It seemed every time I turned around, Rod was getting zapped. He has a great attitude and was the first to laugh it off despite the pain.

Then there are my stories. Somehow, I made it through the eye center construction work without injury or a close call (I rationalized that the mamba in the tree didn't count because we weren't working yet). Leave it to me to feel smug that I had a perfect safety record – until the last day of serious work that is. About mid-morning, I nearly fell off the ramp 20 feet to the ground as my foot got tangled in an extension cord. That was closely followed by nearly seriously burning my hand as I grabbed a stairs handrail joint Rod just welded together! My mild burn was bad enough from my perspective, but by then, I had to share my earlier smugness. Big laughs at my expense!

The other major bonding times were at meals. We ate breakfast, morning and afternoon breaks, lunch and dinner together. Barb lovingly made all of our meals — she always cooked breakfast and dinner when we weren't guests of a missionary family. She also brought us sandwiches for lunch, as well as a morning break snack and more fluids at 10:30! We had wonderful conversations around their table and at the job site.

As their departure got closer, I realized how kind God has been to me in this. Instead of traveling alone and having to figure out life at Bongolo, He gave me the perfect teammates and new friends. He permitted me to adapt to life as part of a team, each of us bringing our strengths and weaknesses. I'm going to miss them and the routines we created. Now that they're gone, I will create a new normal with my buddy and roommate, Ray. There will be a new blend of socializing with increased alone time.

Lessons Learned So Far

1. The most unlikely group can become a team when each person wants to contribute. We have five different personalities that blended together well.

2. Being part of a team takes a lot of pressure off when traveling to and working in a new culture.

3. Rod and I created a special friendship based on trust and vulnerability. I'll cherish this for the rest of my life.

To Ponder

How well do I experience "team" in my life?

Affirmation

I thrive when I'm part of the right team!

What an Amazing Hospital!

One of the highlights of last week was Dr. Keir's tour of the Hospital. Keir, in addition to leading the medical work here, is a general surgeon. He is about 40 years old and married to Joanna. Joanna home schools their children, Sarah (13) and Luke (11), and leads the busy visitor ministry, scheduling and coordinating individual visitors and teams. She also beautifully fulfills the role of medical director's wife in the surrounding villages and Lébamba, enhancing the reputation of Bongolo Hospital in the community. This is their tenth year here. They are kind, thoughtful, and bold witnesses for Christ.

I digress, however, so let's get back to the tour. I'm grateful I had time to settle in and begin to adjust to life here before learning how medical care is delivered American-style but adapted to Gabon. The sprawling campus, mostly one-story with a few two-story hospital buildings, covers an area of about a quarter mile square. The buildings have been constructed as medical needs and the number and variety of doctors here have changed over the decades. There are always two to three buildings and other projects either in the midst of renovation, construction, or in the planning and fundraising stages.

The Hospital is, in many ways, similar to American ones. Excellent care is given in clean, designated rooms. Many departments are the same as those back home: general surgery, pediatrics, eye clinic, maternity, outpatient care, pharmacy, etc. General surgery (laparoscopic and traditional) includes several American specialties. Keir told us the only types of procedures *not* done here are brain, spine, and some heart surgeries.

While there are many similarities to the services back home, there are also a number of stark differences:

- There are a number of critical local specialties we don't usually see in the States: Tuberculosis treatment and quarantine, HIV/AIDS (about 7% of Gabonese have HIV/AIDS, much lower than elsewhere in Africa), and, of course, Africa's biggest killer, malaria.

- Patients don't make advance appointments. They arrive before 8:00 AM Monday through Friday (weekends are for emergency cases only, as well as inpatient care). The vast majority get a ride in an old, beat up "taxi" minivan or truck, or simply walk. They are sorted by level of urgency and type of care needed. They get a number and walk to another building to pay (either cash or through a rudimentary national medical insurance program).

- After that, patients and at least one family member stoically wait *outside* in the courtyard and other waiting areas until it is their turn, sometimes all day. Can you imagine an American waiting outside in the hottest summer day, whether dry or raining, maybe under an awning or not, sitting on hard benches, with no cafeteria or other conveniences? I can't imagine it either.

- There is no air conditioning anywhere in the patient areas except for surgery, and even then sweat often pours down the surgeon's face. Doctors either wear scrubs or standard white coats over slacks and short-sleeved shirts. They are wet with sweat all day, every day.

- Much technology here is old by U.S. hospital standards or non-existent. For example, there are no CT scanners or MRI machines. Infant incubators are made of thin plywood boxes heated beaneath with a light bulb. All of those instruments are too expensive and nearly impossible to maintain from this remote location. Therefore, doctors and surgeons apply modern knowledge, but with creative, old-school doctoring. Nurses record patient information by hand, which is scanned and stored at the end of the day. Patients either bring a handwritten medical log booklet or are given one upon arrival.

- There is no ambulance to transport patients to other hospitals for specialized care not provided here. They only have their own transportation or, on rare occasions, a privately-paid, military-medical helicopter life-flight situation, like we had this week. Thankfully, it was the only one in the last year. The "ambulance" that drove him to the local elementary school sports field was the maintenance director's tiny truck with fold down sides!

- There are no other comparable facilities within hundreds of miles.

- Every patient treated at Bongolo hears about Jesus from a pastor, nurse, or/and a doctor. All patients receive prayer unless they refuse. This is important, since witch doctors still hold a lot of local spiritual power. Last year alone, more than 2,000 people converted to Christianity and began a relationship with our Lord Jesus Christ!

Lessons Learned So Far

1. I'm grateful to be working at this hospital in case I get hurt. Otherwise, I'd be looking at hundreds of miles of dirt-road travel to get to a comparable facility.

2. I pray regularly for physical protection from African diseases foreign to my American body. I'm also grateful for all of my immunizations and daily malaria pill.

3. Even though I'm aware of the risks, I don't worry about getting sick – I'm here on a "mission from God." While this quote from *The Blues Brothers* movie may sound superficial, I remind myself of this truth many times each day.

To Ponder

*What can I learn about to expand
my perspective of life and the world?*

Affirmation

I am actively on a mission from God!

Village Church

I had the chance to worship at a local Christian and Missionary Alliance (C&MA) church, the same denomination as my home church in Pittsburgh. Gabon is a heavily-missionized C&MA country, with churches all over. Ray and I were guests of Dr. Simplice Tchoba, the first Gabonese surgeon to graduate from the training program at Bongolo Hospital. He is a vibrant man in his early-30s, married with four young children, and I enjoyed my time with him.

Church had many similarities and vast differences when compared to my American church. The bottom line is the same Jesus is worshipped and the same Bible is used as the rest of the world. Worship was wonderfully African. What I heard about the singing here is true. The enthusiasm, passion, harmonies, improvisation, and clapping are great to hear and be a part of. While I happily joined in, I felt more than a little stiff. The preaching covered calling people to be trained as pastors and to support the local and national church. This is commonly done at home, too. Announcements and a welcome to first-time visitors came near the end. Two offerings were taken: one for the local assembly and one for the national church.

That's where the similarities ended. Sunday's worship took place at a tiny church in Lébamba. There was no band, just two ladies with a tambourine and a large African "rattle." There were no microphones, but the beautiful singing and clapping were deafening. We sat on narrow wood pews made of wood and our feet rested on a rough concrete floor.

Small lizards and geckos made themselves at home on the side window screens and tapestries. Birds chirped and, at one point, a rooster crowed repeatedly. There was plenty of natural heat, but no air conditioning (have I told you there is no air conditioning here?). There was, however, the luxury of a ceiling fan. The only truly disappointing thing was when the pastor requested it be turned off as it was blowing his papers around!

Also, church lasted 2.5 hours and the service was in French! Thank goodness Simplice often translated. At the end, I had a sore seat, legs, and back, and had sweat through my clothes. I would gladly pay that price again for such an experience!

It's clear worship today was the opposite experience of church at home, except for one thing: Jesus Christ was present and you could sense His love as people worshipped Him. That was just like at home, perhaps even more so. They thanked Ray and me for being there simply because we demonstrated that our God is the same God and can be worshipped in this corner of Africa or back in the States. I hadn't thought of that and am grateful Simplice brought it to my attention!

Lessons Learned So Far

1. I can sit for much longer than I ever thought I could!
2. Church was deeply fulfilling even though I couldn't understand what was being said or sung.
3. A large chunk of time was spent praying over various topics. I liked slowing the service down for this.
4. I would enjoy returning to this "primitive" church environment next week to continue to experience God with my fellow believers. If you'd have asked me that a week ago, I would have said you were crazy. Thank You, Father, for preparing my heart and mind for so many new experiences.

To Ponder

How can I build new experiences into my life?

Affirmation

I am open to new experiences,
especially in areas very important to me!

I realize there has been no construction and "work" update since the first couple of days here. To everyone's stunned delight, this two-month-old project is about three weeks ahead of schedule. That might not sound like a lot, but to put this in perspective, it's not unusual for just this Phase 1 of a Bongolo building project to have taken months instead of weeks to complete. The team from Ohio that got here well before we did built, with local contractor assistance, the frame from scratch, had about 150 25-foot-long steel joists hoisted up to the second floor and roughly positioned, and had part of the roof in place when we arrived. We came prepared to install the roof and, if there was time, hoist the joists into rough position and begin welding them in place. Instead, we started with positioning, every 24 inches, all 150 of the joists, and welded them in place (while strengthening the bridging beneath them). Then, we positioned and welded or screwed large, heavy-duty aluminum corrugated sheets to the joists over the entire floor space. The team following ours was scheduled to do this.

We adapted to the circumstances that we found, something that seems to happen a lot here.

Don't get me wrong. This was all-consuming and exhausting work, done in a dangerous, 20-feet-off-the-ground setting, in over 100-degree weather with 90% plus humidity. We worked in jeans, a t-shirt, safety vest, and hard hat. All day, every day for two work weeks, we sweated so much that our clothing felt like we'd jumped fully clothed into a swimming pool. I literally peeled mine off every night. Personally, I drank about 6-8 liters of water or Gatorade daily and was *still* dehydrated. We got our work done in spite of the conditions.

Another level of flexibility was more personal. A major part of the "after-my-team-left" work I'd been asked to do was to facilitate the transition between construction teams. This didn't happen, however, for the project manager actually cancelled the next team's visit because there was no more work for Americans! Because it's critical that Africans are employed as much as possible, a local general contractor is going to finish the rest of the building, except for specialty work such as installing all of the electric. Even though I would have understood, I don't think I would have been very happy if I were on the team that was cancelled.

Lessons Learned So Far

1. Focused, hard work always pays off somehow. In this case, it has resulted in being substantially ahead of schedule.

2. Adaptability is a much-needed attribute here. We arrived fully prepared for one project and ended up successfully completing a different one.

3. Being ahead of schedule provides for options. Our team was able to also complete other needed projects the last two days we were here.

4. Doing meaningful work is its own reward. Each of us was filled with a sense of accomplishment that we did our work in a God-honoring manner.

To Ponder

When and why is my work most fulfilling?

Affirmation

Flexibility makes life a fulfilling adventure!

Translating and Construction

Since we finished our portion of building the eye center, my "work days" have been spent shadowing the maintenance director, Paul Davis. The plan is for me to run things for a few weeks in February and March so Paul and his wife, Meladee, can have some vacation time. The only breaks they've had have been when Paul was twice back in the States having and recovering from major surgery. I'm excited and honored to help and, if I think about it, nervous about this responsibility.

The Davises have served at Bongolo Hospital for seven years. Paul is a retired union journeyman for General Motors. Whatever Paul didn't know about running a large hospital and living quarters compound when he got here, he had the technical background and experience to figure out on the fly. He leads a crew of eight local men who do everything from lawn care to maintenance service calls. Paul speaks "Frenglish," a blend of French and English, and gets by well much of the time. When he needs to have a more detailed conversation, he typically asks Pastor Serge, the hospital director of administration who heads the non-medical hospital departments, to translate.

This happened today. Paul called a meeting at the job site with Bakary Kamate, the general contractor. The purpose was to discuss and reach an agreement regarding the next phase of the eye center building project. Paul wanted to make sure Bakary understood how to follow the very specific blueprints so there would be no mistakes or work stoppages.

The next phase is to lay concrete footers around the perimeter and inside the structure, so that a ground level concrete subfloor can be poured and interior and exterior concrete block walls can be built. This is because if it can be avoided, nothing here is built from wood because it either rots in the humidity or is eaten by bugs. Bakary speaks just a few words in

English. Paul has worked with him on and off on other building projects over the last seven years and, most of the time, they communicate pretty well and appear to like each other.

It was fascinating for me to observe each of them stating either what he wanted or asking questions. We all paid attention to the speaker as if we could understand him, then turned to Serge for the translation. Working through a translator takes more time and requires patience. The meeting was courteous and business-like. Interestingly, both Paul and the contractor took the opportunity to express other information to clarify and deepen their working relationship.

At the end, Paul was pleased with how the meeting went and I appreciated being included.

Lessons Learned So Far

1. There is always so much to learn! I had previously imagined speaking through a translator, but it was an eye opener to participate in the meeting today.

2. Courteous patience is a beautiful thing.

3. Getting it done in spite of conditions is impressive. Serge was dressed in a suit with shiny loafers, not work boots. It rained last night, so there was mud at the building site. Serge couldn't have cared less that his shoes got muddy and dirty.

To Ponder

How can I slow down and listen better?

Affirmation

*I love to learn new things that
make me a better person!*

As I mentioned, I'm shadowing Paul daily and learning.

Moving people and materials is very important here. The doctors and other missionaries who have cars drive a stick-shift SUV because of the gigantic ruts in all of the dirt roads outside of the compound. Dirt roads are still common everywhere. We have some ruts here, but they're nothing by comparison. Let me briefly describe the work vehicles the maintenance department has, since they are important due to the rugged terrain as well as the work to be done. Nearly all of them are at least 20 years old, yet still get the job done.

The first is a tiny Chevy truck unlike anything I've ever seen. It's similar to a regular truck, but drives on very small tires, seats only two adults, has a six-foot bed and all three sides fold down. This is Paul's day-to-day vehicle. It also has air conditioning – a definite treat in the afternoon! He uses it to drive around the compound, shop for, transport and deliver materials, and to move the guys. I've experienced six riding in the back from project to project – we stand and sit as need be. The Hospital also has a slightly larger Ford pickup that seats five. At the opposite extreme is an ancient dump truck, which is used as a garbage truck on Mondays, Wednesdays, and Fridays. It is also used to transport the fifty-five gallon fuel drums and larger quantities of materials. It's a real blessing!

There are three "fun" small vehicles: the mule and two three-wheelers. I thought they were custom-built African creations, but it turns out they are made in Indiana, U.S. They were shipped here in pieces and reassembled on-site to avoid tens of thousands of dollars in tariffs. The mule is like a golf cart on steroids. It seats two and has a 3-by-4 foot bed. This vehicle doesn't have a gear shift, just forward and reverse with an accelerator, brake, and emergency brake. I wish American golf carts were this cool! The three-wheelers are even more exotic. They only have one seat for the driver, but at least one guy rides in the back as they weave around picking up garbage. The extended handle bars remind me of a hog motorcycle.

My final and favorite maintenance vehicle is the backhoe. Yes, there is a full-sized, American-made backhoe here! I've already used it and can't wait to learn more. It is used for fast digging and moving the gravel and sand used to make concrete. Before the backhoe, the men did significant road repairs (mostly filling in large ruts) by hand. The gravel and cement were shoveled into truck beds and driven to the repair site. Now the backhoe does it in a fraction of the time. The closest Paul has had to a work stoppage was when he suggested they *not* use the backhoe on a road repair. I think he was joking.

Each of these vehicles serves a purpose. They are well-maintained and are vital to the maintenance of the compound buildings and roads.

Lessons Learned So Far

1. Old doesn't mean bad. These work vehicles take a beating but are quite reliable.

2. Thank God I learned to drive a stick shift when I was younger. It's a lot of fun to drive a stick shift after more than 25 years of automatic transmissions.

3. I need to get an international driver's license from AAA for approximately $10. I am limited to driving only in the compound and to the small little village, Dahkar, which is a quarter of a mile away. To drive anywhere else, I'd need either an international license or a Gabonese license.

4. I'm excited to learn to drive strange new vehicles. The mule and backhoe are top of the list for totally different reasons.

To Ponder

What is my attitude towards my means of transportation?

Affirmation

*I confidently apply my driving skills
and habits to new, foreign situations!*

Gradual Adjustments

God is amazing. He knows I learn well when I can slowly adjust to something new instead of being thrown into the deep end (that works too, it's just more stressful). Today was no exception. Let me explain.

God was gracious to allow me to adjust to this exotic place at a slower pace when He saw fit to make me part of a five-person team as opposed to doing this solo. For the first 10 days, our team of five was attached at the hip. We worked together every day, shared every breakfast, lunch, and dinner together, with Barb graciously doing all of the cooking, which was how she viewed her role on the team. We also spent time together out on weekend outings, as well as talking or playing cards most evenings.

When Barb, Rob, and Bobby went home last Wednesday, Ray and I adjusted to working closely together, cooking for ourselves, and having a less hectic evening schedule. Ray, my last Pittsburgh teammate, left for home at 8:00 AM. As I watched him drive towards the air strip for his flight to Libreville, I came face-to-face with being at Bongolo on my own. "And then there was one," a sense of loneliness, would have been a very natural response for me in the past.

This time, however, was different. Instead of gloom, I found myself thinking, "And then there were two" because God is with me, I wept quietly. You'd think crying would have been a woe-is-me reaction of grief and fear at being by myself in the jungle of Africa. Upon quick reflection, I realized my tears were those of gratitude for God's wisdom and love, and for my teammates. Instead of blindly dropping me into an alien situation, God permitted me to gradually learn and adjust, at first with four others, then with Ray.

I smiled through my tears as I turned to go inside, got

my hat and sunglasses, and confidently headed off to work. My next gradual adjustment was underway.

Lessons Learned So Far

1. When I think I'm better off doing something on my own, I will remember that I learn best gradually with a team.

2. I learn gradually a lot more than I think I do!

3. I love being a member of a great team.

4. There is great power of a duo when God is in charge and I am following His orders.

To Ponder

What is going on in my life that
might be a gradual transition?

Affirmation

I learn and adapt quickly,
regardless of the circumstances!

Sand from the River

If I need concrete back home, I could either pick up a few bags of concrete mix at Home Depot or phone a supplier and have a concrete truck come to my site and pour as much as I need. I could also rent a small, portable mixer for a medium-sized job. It's not like that at Bongolo Hospital or many other African projects.

Here, there are no stores like Home Depot and no giant cement trucks. What you do have are raw materials and manpower. For large jobs, such as pouring four inches of concrete at the 50-by-125-foot eye center second floor, using a large, portable mixer is a treat, but they're rare, so that's not a given. What is normal to see is teams of men continually run wheelbarrows of concrete over wood plank ramps, dump their loads, and go back for more until the job is finished, even if it means working all night, which they did.

For smaller projects, such as filling giant, rain-caused ruts in the road or pouring footers as the base of a new building, you mix concrete by hand right there. First, start with the pile of sand and scoop a crater in the center, just like when making a gravy pond in the center of a helping of mashed potatoes. Next, add the right proportion of gravel, cement mix, and water. If you're lucky, there's a hose. Otherwise, you haul buckets of water. Finally, start mixing with a shovel and voila! In 15-20 minutes, you have ready-to-use concrete and you repeat until finished. This is hot, dirty, and exhausting work.

"Where in the middle of the jungle do the materials come from?" you may ask. That's an excellent question. Everything is locally sourced one way or another. Getting the sand was the most interesting part for me. At least here, it is dug from the river by hand about a half mile outside of the hospital grounds. At the bottom of Bongolo Falls, the Luetsi

River turns to the right and there is a large, curved "lagoon" area to the left. Because of the Falls, sand is continually replenished. This digging and loading lagoon is surrounded by lush foliage, trees, and bamboo groves. It's beautiful and is also a community bathing and clothes-washing area.

Here's how they get the sand. Men pole their two-by-20-foot long wooden dugout canoes — yes, dugout canoes — into the shallow digging area, jump into the waist-deep river, and with a wooden bucket start scooping sand and dumping it, bucket after bucket, into the canoe (along with a lot of water). A little while later, when the canoe is filled and nearly ready to sink, they gingerly climb in and carefully pole back to shore, riding the slow current. The slightest imbalance would tip the canoe and they would need to start over.

They guide their dugouts as close to the edge of the beach as possible, and get back out to scoop out the sand, again bucket by bucket, onto a growing mound. Customers, with trucks of all sizes, drive right to the water's edge to be loaded. The sand is shoveled by several men into the bed of the truck. What a process! It takes days to make large mounds. Talk about a group of tough, amazingly fit men of all shapes and sizes.

We needed lots of sand for the eye center project and for patching the roads of the compound, so Paul and I, along with 13-year-old Luke Thelander, took the dump truck and backhoe to the river where Western met Central African. Paul loaded 24 tons of sand — eight dump truck loads, over half of all the sand there, which I delivered to various locations around the compound. In between loads, Paul used the backhoe to help the sand merchants, which I admired. He drove as far into the river as he could, then dropped the front shovel and backed up, pulling sand that was washing away farther up onto solid ground so that there would be more to sell, providing them with a couple of days' worth of free work in just a few minutes. He didn't charge them for this — and I can't tell you if we got a discount on our purchase. I think Paul simply figured his actions were part of demonstrating Christ's love through serving and making friends.

Lessons Learned So Far

1. Entrepreneurs are all alike, whether in Bongolo or the U.S.
2. "Where there's a will, there's a way" is especially true here.
3. While I'm in awe of the physical strength and endurance of the working men, I would not want to pay the price to be like them.
4. Using our resources to help others makes friends and shows them Jesus in us.

To Ponder

How are "old ways" good things in my life?

Affirmation

I admire and emulate the hard work of others!

Birthday Reflections

Monday, February 15th was my 53rd birthday. I was very grateful for all the well-wishes and greetings! My tradition for many years has been to take off work on my birthday and spend the day however I want. I've found this indulgence to be physically, emotionally, and spiritually fulfilling, so I did the same thing this year. As far as I know, Paul Davis is the only one who knows, and that's only because I asked if it was all right not to work today. Before saying, "Yes, of course," Paul being Paul had to first tease me that he'd put together a specific, high-priority Doug-list for that day!

First, I slept in until a whopping 7:00 AM. After my quiet time (Bible study and commentary, and *My Utmost for His Highest*), I took time to reflect on various significant topics, such as:

- What is God's plan for me regarding long-term missions work? *(No firm answer; I'm open to His plan for me wherever and whatever that is.)*

- How do I figure this out? *(Praise God before I get answers; intentional trust and surrender that God is in control; worry is lack of faith.)*

- At the halfway point of my trip, how well am I fulfilling my mission here at Bongolo? *(I think I'm on track.)*

On a more lighthearted note, I've been jotting down lists of what I miss, what I don't miss, and what I'm grateful for about my life in America. I've chuckled at some of these and want to share them. The lists are in no particular order:

I miss: my closest friends and family; my dishwasher and garbage disposal; clothes dryer; Modern Café laughter; American restaurants; my small Bose Bluetooth speaker; fresh vegetables; American stores, especially Home Depot and a great supermarket; church in English; YMCA CrossFit; fast, reliable Internet (can't easily upload/download, watch videos); my cat, Tutu; hugs; Super Bowl commercials and parties; birthday week celebrations.

While overall I'm content, it would be nice to have them.

I don't miss: being a slave to my cell phone; voluminous emails/texts; winter in any way, shape or form; the hectic pace of American life; watching movies at night; winter (it's worth repeating!); angry, impatient drivers; craft IPA beer; TVs everywhere; the noise; pollution, consumerism, materialism, and the news.

I'm grateful for: Most of the long-term missionaries at Bongolo have told me that this remote hospital can be a challenging place to live. I'm starting to understand what they mean. With that in mind, I'm grateful I brought lots of bug spray and suntan lotion; my cell phone (for photos, WhatsApp, Facebook, Skype and email); Bluetooth head phones; Kindle books; Rosetta Stone French; laptop; lots of downloaded music and digital audio books; puzzles for the missionaries (a couple were still available, so I'm working on *Flags of the World*, one that Mom and Dad donated that I'm sure I did several times growing up).

I'm also grateful to have consistent electricity; safe drinking water; a Western bathroom, kitchen and bed; box fans; the ability to instantly communicate with everyone (as long as I have Wi-Fi), an attractive comfortable place to stay; enough good food; growing friendships, especially with Paul; that which was at first alien and scary has become more normal.

I am beginning to love life here.

Most significantly, I'm continually grateful for the on-going love and financial support of my family, friends, and ACAC church family. They are tangibly making it possible for me to be working to my capacity without worry here at

Bongolo. Without them, I'd likely be pondering how to manage severe loneliness.

Lessons Learned So Far

1. I can happily live without so much that I previously thought was normal and necessary.

2. Contentment is a disciplined attitude that stems from a decision to be so.

3. Gratitude is easy when I put my mind and heart to it!

To Ponder

*How often do I reflect on the simple things
for which I should be grateful?*

Affirmation

I am so grateful for God's provision in my life!

Praying for Electricity

There is a major electrical problem at Bongolo Hospital this week. I have to admit, until I got here, I've never thought much about electricity. After all, in America it's always there unless there's a bad storm or something equally unusual. Even then, if the power goes out at my home, the worst part is lighting a few candles for a while, then resetting the blinking clocks on my microwave, coffee maker, oven, and alarm clock when power comes back on. While this is rare at home, it's still a big pain when it happens.

"Big pain" takes on a whole new meaning here. It's no understatement that every aspect of the hospital relies on electricity, from surgery lights and monitors to premature baby incubators; from the TB and AIDS wards to the air conditioned medicine warehouse and pharmacy; from the emergency room to cooling the central electrical hub. It's the same the quarter of a mile away up the steep hill to the Station, where we all live. The Station's office, computers and Internet also rely on consistent electricity. Our refrigerators can only keep food cold and frozen for so long in the jungle heat without power. When the power is out, the ceiling fans and box fans don't keep the heat and humidity down or the bugs away.

The quest for consistent electricity has been a continuous battle. When we're winning, life is pretty normal by American standards. When we're losing, however, it can be fatal for patients in the middle of an operation, those relying on oxygen machines to breathe, or premature babies who will die if their incubators fail. Hence, consistent electricity is a big deal.

Our regular power is generated by the government-owned hydroelectric power plant located three quarters of a mile from the hospital at the top of Bongolo Falls. The potential for electricity was one of the reasons Donald Fairley, the original founding missionary at Bongolo, began the mission here. In the early 1950s, he and more than 100 workers and technicians imported 19 tons of equipment and, over a two-month period, transported it 250 grueling jungle miles to Bongolo. For the following eighteen months, they built the first plant by hand which provided the mission compound with electricity for forty years. In 1992, a new, larger, government-owned power plant took over, which extended electricity to nearby towns and villages. Their plant is located on Hospital-owned land, so the arrangement is they don't pay us rent and we don't pay for electricity.

Even though this is mutually-beneficial, their power is unfortunately quite unstable. Stoppages occur almost daily and they often produce inconsistent voltage, causing surges and other problems. The current problem (no pun intended) at the power plant is that two of their four turbines are broken. The last time this happened, it wasn't until three were broken that the government finally sent in repair technicians. We are praying it will be different this time.

Many years ago, the Hospital bought generators as emergency back-ups. They get a lot of use. Since I've been here, I've either helped maintain, inspect, or operate all three of them. The main one is the newest and largest. It can run the entire Hospital and Station for a while, but the need has outgrown its capacity to the point of possible breakdown. While it was more than adequate ten years ago, today the usage has increased dramatically. It is actually half the size of the replacement one they are hoping to purchase in the near future. The other two are a World War II-era monster dedicated to Surgery and Recovery, and a smaller, more modern one for Maternity's needs. Those two are only used if and when the primary generator fails. The World War II generator is on its last legs.

Because of the turbine problem at the hydroelectric plant, we have been operating our main backup generator for hours at a time on and off for the last several days. This is extremely expensive in terms of the cost of diesel fuel and time consuming for staff, since each of the eight 55 gallon barrel is filled at the only gas station, about 15 minutes away in Lébamba. The estimate is that it costs $1,000 a day to run the generator.

Eventually, high usage overheats the generator, causing it to shut off. We got through the weekend because the hospital slows down on Saturdays and Sundays. Yesterday and today, however, were a different story. The drain on the generator got so bad it continually overheated and shut down. Paul shut off power to the Station homes to divert the electricity to the hospital. Orders were circulated throughout the Hospital to turn off every unneeded light and machine until the crisis passed. This helped us limp through until the power plant came back on line. This kind of thing is unheard of in the States.

Unfortunately, we don't see any relief from this in the near future. In fact, it won't be surprising, based on past events, if it gets worse for a time. We have asked for (and been told "Yes") that we will have regular electricity from 9:00-5:00 during the day when the Hospital is at its peak usage, then it will be shut off and diverted elsewhere. Therefore, we will need to run the generator at night. This statement from the power company has already been as unreliable as the electricity itself. The reality is we really need a much larger generator, but those funds (about $350,000) are not yet available.

Lessons Learned So Far

1. I am very grateful for ceiling and box fans! Without them, it's so humid (near 100% all the time) and hot here (100s during the day and still mid-70s at night) that I would sweat all night trying to sleep.

2. Electricity rationing requires cooperation. It's pretty much an honor system at the Hospital and the Station to minimize electric use when need be.

3. A silver lining is that I can use rationing to my advantage to get more sleep. I can turn off my lights, go to bed earlier, and get up before dawn when it's cooler.

To Ponder

What might I voluntarily ration that would benefit others?

Affirmation

Making the best of things is an exciting challenge!

Good Water

I've done my best to obey the health dictum of drinking eight glasses of water every day for years and have done pretty well overall. That's the equivalent of drinking about a half-gallon of water each day. Some people question whether they could really do this for various reasons.

I now have a different question: Where does the water come from and is it safe to drink? If you're like me, you've never spent a lot of time thinking about this, any more than you do about flipping a light switch. I am now intimately aware of the answer to this question, at least as it refers to the water used at Bongolo Hospital.

The Hospital and Station sit a short half mile from the Luetsi River, and Bongolo Falls is the source of their drinking water. The falls are a long series of step-down rapids that crescendos at the final falls, where they turn into 800 feet or so of crashing water. It's really beautiful, especially during the rainy season. A steady supply of water has never been a problem. The issue has been to create safe drinking water, at first for a small number of missionaries and their families, but today for a team of about 15 and their families, about 100 hospital staff, and a couple of hundred patients a day.

Just like water elsewhere, harmful bacteria naturally live in the rivers and streams. Additionally, villagers still use those water sources for bathing and washing clothes. The good news is there's not any significant industry anywhere nearby to add chemical and toxic pollutants. Supply is not the issue, safety is. So, the question remains: How to make the water safe to drink? Over the 80-plus years since the first missionaries settled here, solutions such as boiling water and ceramic purifying filters have been used and periodically upgraded. Fortunately, starting in 2011, Bongolo installed a small, modern water treatment system. Here's how it works.

Step one is to get water up from the river 200 feet below. Two electric pumps are anchored in a still portion of the river near the top of the Falls. The water is pumped up through long hoses into a small block structure called the Silt House. This single-story, 15-by-30 foot building houses two separate block and concrete reservoirs, each about six feet deep. Water slowly moves from pool to pool, depositing silt and other heavier-than-water materials on the bottom. The cleaner water stays closer to the top. At the end of this sequence, the somewhat cleaner water flows about 25 feet downhill into the pump house, another single-story, 15-by-30 foot block building.

The technology at the pump house is quite modern and sophisticated. Like many non-hospital improvements here, the equipment was either donated or bought with raised funds. In this case, it was donated by a generous U.S. company. There is a large, high-tech micro-filter machine, three large sand filters, three chemical vats, two more large storage tanks, and a chlorine system. The water that emerges at the end of this process is pumped either directly down to the hospital at the bottom of the steep hill, or up to a water tower (tiny compared to the ones that we see in American towns) for use upon demand.

Amazingly, the water produced there is at least as clean as tap water in American cities. At the Station, the missionary residents and visitors can add an optional final purifying step by pouring containers of tap water into a two-gallon ceramic filter. The water that comes out the twist tap at the bottom is even purer, so much so that everyone here takes daily multi-vitamins with trace minerals, because all of them are removed during the filtering. For years, these ceramic filters were what everyone used to create clean water, so nearly all of the missionaries still use their ceramic filters, even though they technically no longer need to do so. This is simply a safety habit (and possibly a taste preference) formed over the years. Visitors are taught to use the ceramic-filtered water, so we joined in. But this is time consuming and tedious, especially with the volume we drank, so after the first two weeks, I decided to trust Paul's assurance that the tap water is perfectly safe to drink. Thank God, I've not once felt the slightest stomach or bowel upset. It's just like being at home, and quite frankly, I like the taste better.

Part of my training to take over for Paul has been to monitor and maintain this system. The water treatment system requires continuous care and supervision. Chlorine is manually added three times per week, gauges are monitored for any changes, and the equipment needs to be backwashed (cleaned out) at least once a week to keep the system as pure as possible. Except for electricity, no other system here is anywhere near as important as creating, maintaining, and monitoring safe drinking water. The last thing I want is to be responsible for people getting sick, so I've taken this responsibility seriously.

Lessons Learned So Far

1. Drinking at least eight glasses of water a day here is a piece of cake. The other end of that spectrum has been the bigger challenge: staying hydrated. On a "non-physical" day, I find I drink two to three times more water than I do at home.

2. *Appropriate* risk usually pays off. I'm so glad I listened to and trusted Paul. After tentatively taking just a few sips over a couple of days, I started drinking the tap water. First of all, I think it tastes way better than the ceramic-filtered product. Second, it's more convenient. Third, it has the trace minerals the ceramic-filtered water doesn't, so my body is healthier.

3. Different people value different things. Even though many of the long-time residents may know intellectually that the

tap water is safe, they still opt for ceramic-filtered water. They know without a doubt they won't get sick, and they also think it tastes better, I guess. There's absolutely nothing wrong with that.

To Ponder

How well do I do at not taking something or somebody who is important for granted?

Affirmation

I gratefully drink as much water as my body needs!

But It's a Wet Heat

"But it's a dry heat" has become the stuff of legend in the American Southwest. They seem to use this phrase no matter how hot and dry these desert regions get. Nobody in the jungle makes any such statements concerning the typical 90-100 plus degree daytime temperatures and constant high humidity here. Even though the phrase, "jungle paradise" would certainly be appropriate, it's not surprising when people here complain about the weather. That seems to be a typical gripe everywhere. Not everybody does, mind you, but I've heard weather gripes from missionaries, patients, and native local residents alike:

- "It's so hot today that I can't stand the idea of going outside!"

- "Wow, I'm melting in this humidity!"

- "I can't wait for the dry season!" (when there's much less rain and daytime temps peak in the 80s. Of course, then they'll complain about how dry and dusty everything is. Some will even complain about how cold it is!)

This complaining irritates me here just like back in the States. That's because there's only one solution: move away! Back home, I sometimes find myself whining when it's 40 degrees and raining. But overall, I've done my best to live by Eleanor Roosevelt's philosophy: "There is no such thing as bad weather, only inappropriate clothing." Embrace it or move!

Believe it or not, there are four distinct seasons here, even though Bongolo is barely south of the equator. They're not as diverse as the northeastern United State's seasons, but there really *are* differences. The seasons are: dry, rainy, mini-dry, and mini-rainy, in that order.

Bongolo's Seasons

Mini-Dry Season. When I arrived in late January, southern Gabon was on the tail end of its two-month, mini-dry season (typically December and January). Daytime high temperatures are in the high 90s into the 100s, with lots of hazy sunshine and near 100% humidity. The nights stay hot — often only down into the 80s. Some of the days were beautifully cloudless with a million stars out at night. In fact, it only rained twice during our first three weeks. One was a 30-minute "shower" that was a real downpour by Western standards. The second was a dramatic three-hour, night-time thunderstorm, complete with dazzling nearby lightning strikes.

Rainy Season. The rainy season started a little bit late this year in mid-February. The first storm was a giant all-nighter that continued into the following morning. The amount of thunderous rain was truly unbelievable. We'd been told about these storms, but the actual experience was incredible. There were lots of spectacular, close lightning strikes so bright that they hurt my eyes. I can't help but wonder how often the common ungrounded metal roofs and metal electric poles get hit (by the way, they can't use wood for poles because they rot and the termites and ants eat them too quickly). The daily, late-afternoon rains typically start at the end of January or the beginning of February, but this hasn't happened yet this year, likely due to this being an El Nino year.

Dry Season. The dry season is usually from June through September. This is their winter and it is less rainy and cooler, with daytime highs in the low 80s and low 70s at night. It's also cloudier. I've heard this can cause depression symptoms, but I don't think it's the mind-numbing dreariness of Pittsburgh or Seattle winters. On the funny side, many locals put on coats when it stays "cold." One of our doctors, a pediatrician, grew up here as a missionary kid. She remembers once when it actually got down all the way into the middle 60s!

Mini Rainy Season. October and November typically bring a return of higher temperatures and humidity, as well as lots of rain.

A Few Editorial Comments

Gutters. The gutters on the homes and buildings are gigantic because it's common for 3 to 5 inches of rain to fall in a couple of hours.

Mud. After a torrential overnight rain, deep road mud is a major problem. Amazingly, by early afternoon, the ground is nearly dried out! The hilly terrain is a big drainage factor, as is the lack of paved areas. Of course, sunny and high-90s doesn't hurt either.

Wind. There isn't any wind here to speak of through-out the year. Perhaps the explanation lies in the inland and dramatically hilly terrain. However, there is a surprisingly wonderful light breeze much of the day. It is not enough to move a flag at the top of a pole, but enough to provide much-needed relief from the heat. The only moderate wind I've experienced so far comes before the rain gets serious, and stops when the rain starts, resulting in slow-moving storms that last a while.

Current Weather Patterns. Pretty much every morning has been the same so far: misty fog in the hospital valley from dawn until about 8:30. Then the sun burns off the fog and comes out for the rest of the day. It's commonly partially cloudy or a little bit hazy – but definitely not the scorching sun of Florida or Arizona. Considering the high, humid temperatures, that makes a big difference.

Daily Temperature Patterns. So far, temperatures have been in the low 80s by 8:00 AM, up to about 90 in the shade by lunch time, high 90s into the 100s in the middle of the afternoon, mid-80s at 6:00 PM, and gradual cooling into the low or mid-70s overnight. Then it starts all over again.

On a lighter note, it has been fun to show my new African friends photographs of snow, snow plows, and people shoveling. They say, "Wow!", nod, and smile with absolutely no earthly idea what I'm talking about.

To Ponder

How much do I complain about the weather?

Affirmation

*I make the best of my weather and
enjoy it as much as possible!*

Another Bumpy Ride

Other than something to do with a sports team and the weather, what is the other major "First World" complaint you can't avoid in the northeast United States, especially during the winter? Yup: Potholes. I'll never complain about a pothole again. The paved and generally well-maintained American roads are just fine with me.

The sparse population in Gabon, the Third World economy, and lethargic government mean that good roads are few and far between. The few paved roads have been built by Chinese companies, mostly as part of their government oil, mining, and timber contracts. It makes me wonder how they were going to get their raw materials out of the jungle otherwise, so it was a win-win scenario. Bongolo hired one of these crews a few years ago to build an unpaved curving road around the south side of the hospital for easier access, and that road has held up beautifully.

Like the weather, road conditions and driving are more dramatic than back in the States. Except for two hills at Bongolo and a small stretch in the central shopping portion of Lébamba three miles away, all of the local roads outside of Bongolo are dirt, leaving them very vulnerable to rain run-off.

Here are a few general road observations:

- All roads are bumpy rough, even on a good day.

- Every car is coated with the red dust of Gabon.

- It's very hilly here, so when there's a heavy rain, the water has to drain somewhere, and where better than a vegetation-free road? The result is that ruts are quickly created and they get bigger and deeper after each rain.

- Since Gabon is a former French colony, cars are offi-cially driven on the right side of the road. However...

- The rutted roads have created an "anything goes" driving culture. Mile after mile, vehicles zigzag from right to left and back in an attempt to avoid or to straddle the ruts and puddles. The easiest "paths" emerge in the form of worn tire tracks and savvy drivers follow them – until the ruts get too big and the path shifts accordingly.

- One slip and your vehicle slams down into a rut or mud puddle, possibly getting stuck and or damaged.

- Guard rails are unheard of – cars can easily careen off the roads down into deep ditches or small ravines.

- Drivers usually pause to wait for an oncoming vehicle to pass so they can navigate these pathways. Most drivers wave their appreciation.

- The private "taxis" are more aggressive, which must be customary worldwide!

- All of the taxis and most of the private vehicles are beat-up looking older models.

- There are a few newer, nicer looking cars and trucks, but I'm guessing they don't stay that way for long.

- There is no such thing as AAA road assistance, and cell service is intermittent outside of towns and larger villages. So, if you break down or are in an accident, you're pretty much on your own.

- Many SUV's and trucks are equipped with winches so they can pull themselves out of mud holes and giant ruts.

- Because I don't have an international driver's license, I've been a continual passenger outside of our compound, so I've gotten pretty good at managing the butt-pounding, up and down, side-to-side bumping. It's a lot like when you ride a bike and have to hit a hole, you hold on hard to your handle bars and use your legs to push yourself off of the seat so your arms and legs absorb the blow instead of your back and *derriere* (the actual French word for *behind,* as it turns out).

- I wish there was a chiropractor here!

- When the road is bad enough for long enough, the local mayor or some other official finally sends out a work crew, but they don't seem to be in a hurry to do this. For example, the last two Sundays, I've wanted to visit a village church with one of the missionaries, but the road and a small bridge about 20 minutes from here have been impassable. Maybe this week I can make it.

As bad as the roads have been, I've been told they are way better than years ago. It's hard to imagine that. Thank you, God, for the improvement!

Lessons Learned So Far

1. It's amazing what I take for granted as "normal."
2. The phrase from my first couple of weeks came back to me as I considered the road situation here versus in the States: "It's a First World problem."
3. We in the West are so incredibly blessed as it relates to the infrastructure.
4. I can't help but wonder how many of our so-called "problems" would go away with a shift in perspective.

To Ponder

How do I handle "the bumps, mud holes, and ruts" of life?

Affirmation

I absorb all blows and recover!

Proper Introductions

Pastor Serge Boueni is a man you want to know. His business card reads, "Directeur, Hospital de Bongolo." He's the overall leader of Bongolo Hospital, and has been here for 18 years. He is responsible for every aspect of the 158-bed hospital, from medical to human resources, and facilities to medicine storage. I'd heard of Serge for a long time, and briefly crossed paths with him a couple dozen times since arriving at Bongolo. He is jovial, yet serious, and brings a calming, commanding presence. He is also a wonderfully bold Christian. "Jesus Est Seigneur" — Jesus is Savior — is also on his card. You don't find that on too many American business cards inside or outside of the church. Recently, I had the great fortune of spending most of a day one-on-one with him.

Pastor Serge is the ultimate networker. I've been told by several people here and back home that he knows "everybody," and not just at Bongolo or in Lébamba. He is known throughout Gabon and surrounding countries. He confirmed this when he told me a story. Once, he was driving to Libreville, Gabon's capital about 350 miles to the northwest, which is usually an 8-to-10 hour drive. Some visitors on their way home to the States were with him. Over and over, cars would flash their lights and pedestrians would wave at the car. One of the visitors finally asked why this was happening. Serge, with a smile on his face, told them it's because everybody knows him.

Of his many duties, one of the more pleasant ones is to introduce new permanent missionaries and long-term visitors, such as myself, to the local leadership. He takes them to meet the Mayor of Lébamba, the Chief of Police, and the Prefect, the regional representative of the provincial governor. Why? Consider small-town life in America. There, local leaders want to know everything that's going on. Who's coming and going?

Where are real and potential trouble spots? Who's causing problems? What are our opportunities for growth? Next, add in the sensation caused by the arrival of a person there to contribute somehow to the greater community. They not only want to know they are living nearby, but want to meet them and check them out. Lébamba's leaders are just like that.

Here are some of the differences to small-town America:

- No one speaks English. French is the official and dominant language. Most locals also speak at least one tribal language, such as Nzebi.

- Serge made photocopies of my passport and visa so my identity could be circulated especially to the gendarmerie (police) force.

- We went to three separate buildings in various parts of Lébamba.

- These offices and buildings were nicer than anywhere else I've been, apart from Bongolo's compound, but that's not saying a whole lot.

- The only women I saw, except for one gendarmerie, were clearly either administrative or cleaning staff.

These experiences were fascinating.

Lessons Learned So Far

1. Yet again, having a translator fluent in the local languages makes all the difference.

2. I'm trusting God for protection from identity theft: I'm nervous my passport information is out there.

3. Being proactive makes a lot of sense just in case I wind up in a difficult situation of some type. Today brought to mind the cliché, "A stitch in time saves nine."

To Ponder

*How might meeting key people
help my life (or the lives of others)?*

Affirmation

I am proactive and forward thinking!

Proper Introductions (continued)

Hospital director, Pastor Serge Boueni, wears many hats. One of his roles is to grow and enhance the positive reputation of Bongolo Hospital, whether at the Hospital, in the surrounding towns and villages, in Libreville, or in other countries. For example, for the next two weeks, he will be teaching an advanced hospital administration course in neighboring Cameroon. His task with me, however, has been more mundane — to introduce me to three important local and regional men: the Chief of Police, the Mayor of Lébamba, and the regional Prefect, who represents the governor of this province.

Perhaps mundane isn't the right word. Insignificant may be better to an American way of thinking. After all, who cares whether one more person is in the area? But neither word is appropriate in this instance. Being presented to the local leadership helps to keep good relationships intact, demonstrates respect for local leadership, and provides an opportunity to discuss any current issue on either side. Being presented also helps the Hospital. It's important for these leaders to know that Christians, mainly from America, voluntarily give up their lives for a while, pay to travel for days to get here, and pay for food and lodging while they work hard for free on behalf of Gabon and Bongolo Hospital (Note: my trip has been generously supported by many friends and by my church, ACAC. As part of this blessing, I am able to pay to live and work here at Bongolo).

This type of volunteerism is hard for people over here to relate to, and explaining it to local leaders goes a long way to eliminate a major concern that I heard for the first time while applying for my Gabonese visa: the fear of taking away very limited work from Africans. Therefore, it is important to demonstrate that visitors like me, or like a surgeon who comes for two weeks to teach the African surgical residents, are coming to give. We are taking nothing from Gabon; we are here to give on behalf of Christ Jesus to teach Africans how to fish, so to speak.

Our first meeting was with the Chief of Police for Lébamba and the surrounding villages. He is a tall man by Gabonese standards (about six feet), and is in his 50s from his appearance. We waited a few minutes for him to finish another meeting, and then we were escorted into his plain office. Serge introduced me in French and handed him a dossier (green 11-by-17 inch paper folded in half). After pleasantries were exchanged, Serge told him who I was, why I was at Bongolo, and how long I'd be staying. They discussed this while I sat quietly, not understanding much of the conversation.

When that wound down, I asked if was okay for me to ask a question. I think this surprised both of them! It was permissible, so I inquired about the chief's biggest law enforcement challenges. They were typical: having people understand what the gendarmerie's role is and to cooperate; deal with the occasional drunk and disorderly situation; and intervene in domestic disputes. Crime as we know it is unusual, it turns out. The major outcome of this meeting was that my name and picture would be circulated to his gendarmeries so that they would be aware that I am officially here and working at Bongolo.

Next was the Mayor of Lébamba, Omer Moukokpo. His office is across town in a large, faded-yellow building that an American would think had seen better days. It is actually in very good condition by local standards. The mayor's office is on the second floor, and we were offered seats in his (surprisingly) air conditioned waiting area. After about 10 minutes of waiting, the mayor arrived and we were ushered into his office. It was considerably nicer than the police chief's. I almost smiled when the mayor, dressed in slacks, a dress shirt, and sport coat, bounded up from his desk chair with a big smile to greet us. "What a typical politician," I thought, "gregarious and charming, yet serious when we got down to business."

Again, Pastor Serge presented me in French to considerable nodding on the mayor's part. He was eager to answer my questions, which were slow pitches down the middle of the plate. "What are your biggest opportunities and goals? What are your biggest hurdles?" His answers were typical of most politicians. He wants to provide consistent electricity, good drinking water, and safe streets. I did not get the sense that he had any concrete plan to accomplish these, however. Prior to becoming mayor two years ago, he worked in a different branch of the government.

The final stop was to the prefect's office in yet another part of Lébamba. The prefect, Yves Yassima, is the provincial governor's local representative. He is in charge of the mayor, police chief, and another local official who is in charge of the surrounding small villages. The prefect reports up to a regional official who then reports to the governor. His office, as it befits the senior local leader, was by far the most impressive of the three offices. The walls were freshly painted and it was more spacious. He wore a beautiful dress shirt with cuff links.

He is also a good professional friend of Serge's, and the mutual affection and respect were evident from the start. After being presented, our conversation revolved around my questions about his role, his goals, the role of taxes (new in the last few years when the oil money dried up), and racial and religious tensions (there are none as far as he was concerned). My final question was, "What one thing would you change if you could?" His answer was really interesting. As part of the national Gabonese goal to become more self-sufficient, he wants to increase the farming, production and sale of two crops that are imported from Cameroon so that the local economy could be more self-supporting. One is palm oil, and I didn't catch the second, unfortunately.

While all three leaders were of interest for various reasons, I found the prefect the most intriguing of the three. He clearly cares about his responsibilities and has a vision for moving forward. During this time, it was also clear that Pastor Serge is passionate about and enjoys the networking aspect of his ministry on behalf of God at Bongolo Hospital.

Lessons Learned So Far

1. Being presented is a pretty cool experience. It feels good. We should somehow incorporate this idea more into life in the States.

2. We should all be presented in French or another language other than English to prevent ego growth. My head couldn't really grow because I couldn't understand much of what was being said!

3. My French learning efforts are paying off, however, as I understood more of their conversations than I would have a month ago!

4. Building business relationships is just as important here as at home.

To Ponder

*Where would it be helpful for me
to be presented (by another person)?*

Affirmation

I am worthy of being presented!

What's for Dinner?

Do you eat to live or live to eat? I love healthy, delicious food, especially when made by someone who loves to prepare it. I can cook many things, but I'm no chef. I am, however, a world-class assistant! I'm great at cutting veggies, mixing, stirring, cleaning up, and doing dishes. Other than that, I'm definitely an eat-to-live guy. On the surface, that's good when living in remote Africa as I'm still working out how to get the most enjoyment out of meals. I waited a while before writing this, so let me explain.

The myth of the jungle is that with all of the sunshine, rural conditions and plenty of rain, there should be lots of farming and available produce. People imagine cleared, culti-vated fields resplendent with all kinds of produce. While there is some local farming, it is predominantly the small subsistence variety, and the local available produce is very limited. From what I've been told, the mold, bacteria, ants, and other bugs get the best of non-native crops. Additionally, the cleared jungle regrows so quickly that it's hard to keep it at bay.

Thus, locals eat a diet heavy in carbs, including lots of bread, rice, and the popular root of the manioc plant, which has no apparent nutritional value except it makes one feel full. Unfortunately, it tastes like a pencil eraser. To learn more about the local food options, I reached out for culinary advice to the closest available experts, the English-speaking missionar-ies who have lived here for several years. They have confirmed the variety is limited, especially when it comes to fresh meat, vegetables, and fruit. Chocolate is rare and ice cream (that hasn't been frozen and thawed and frozen again) even more so.

The Annual Food Order

The missionaries have come up with an answer to this,

however. I've been blessed to be a guest at many of their homes and they have all served delicious, creative *American* meals. That's right, American meals. I've been quite surprised by this, but it's not just a special night for visitors; it's how they eat. While they shop locally for fresh foods and some other items, it seems all of them here attempt to recreate U.S. menus as much as possible. So, when I've been a guest for dinner and they prepare these great meals, I've felt guilty that they were sharing scarce food with me. I finally mentioned this and was relieved to find out that a separate portion of Bongolo's annual food order is just for visitors. I wasn't sure I'd heard clearly. Annual food order?

It's exactly what it sounds like: one all-or-nothing opportunity every year to order specific food from America. It's hard to imagine shopping just once a week, let alone once a year. I live by myself back home and I'm at the supermarket three to four times a week, It's a fact, however, that they receive American food items once each year. Visitors bring treats — we certainly did — but these are only periodic and in small quantities.

The shopping is through a U.S.-based supplier that specializes in missionary food orders, and they offer a 35,000-item online catalog. I can't even begin to imagine the breadth and scope of that catalog. With that in mind, everybody orders a year's worth of all of the standard, non-perishable items many families buy at the local food store in the States. A few examples I've seen are breakfast cereals, all kinds of sweet and salty snacks, pasta, spices, sauce, canned olives, ethnic meal mixes, baby formula, cake and brownie mixes and, of course, peanut butter and jelly. Additionally, they order non-food items, such as laundry detergent, bathroom products, personal hygiene items, diapers and wipes, and make-up. Part of the purchase cost is their portion of shipping what they buy.

Everybody's order arrives via a large container (like

the ones pulled by 18-wheeler tractor trailers). Planning takes place in late spring and the order is placed by the early summer deadline. Everything is then shipped to the staging area in the Cleveland, Ohio area and carefully packed. Because this typically doesn't fill an entire container, other larger personal items are also ordered. The container is also filled with hospital equipment and supplies, specialized building and maintenance materials, motors and replacement parts, stoves, washing machines, dryers, and small appliances.

The filled container leaves Ohio in September, bound for an ocean-going ship enroute for Libreville, Gabon. After its time at sea, it is off-loaded onto a large truck and driven to Bongolo. The entire process takes nearly six months, so Thanksgiving and Christmas are truly a time of celebration and gratitude.

Local Food Options: The Bad News

While importing food is safe, familiar, comforting, and delicious, the adventurous food part of me finds it boring and limiting. After all, we're in Africa! The peoples there have successfully eaten local meals here for thousands of years. There must be all kinds of ethnic recipes and concoctions, especially with there being so many Africans from other nearby countries. It only makes sense to identify healthy local options regardless of how strange sounding they might be.

So, what's available locally? Unfortunately, all of the Lébamba shops seem to carry identical non-perishable food merchandise, which is really frustrating. For example, they all carry the same brands of canned peas, green beans, corn (I know that corn is not a veggie but it acts like one here) and mixed vegetables. They also carry canned potatoes and the dreaded canned carrots. They stock an even smaller assortment of frozen veggies and frozen meat as well. There's a lot of chicken, fresh eggs, a little beef, and assorted other regional meats. If we're lucky, there are real potatoes and imported apples that closely resemble and taste like small Golden Delicious apples. It seems only one wholesale supply truck arrives in town and sells some of everything to each of a dozen small stores. Where's the competition? Other than being isolated, this doesn't make a lot of sense to me. I want to learn more.

Then there are the fresh food vendors on the streets of Lébamba who offer a similarly uniform small assortment of fresh fruits, such as plantains, lemons, imported and local tomatoes, as well as the occasional bananas and small watermelons. In the vegetable department, there are colorful, tiny, and very hot peppers. There are also small onions, tomatoes, and the occasional cabbage. They also have several types of leafy greens, such as manioc, which I'm dying to try raw (I'm not a big fan of cooked greens, unfortunately). But the strong recommendation is not to eat them raw due to the taste as and generally unsanitary growing conditions. I like raw greens, especially for blending and in salads, but so far, I'm not willing to risk potential days of food poisoning agony to find out.

Local Food Options: The Good News

All of that is the bad news. The *good news* is the meat and fruit I eat is fresh, organic, and incredibly delicious. Tomatoes, eggs, and bananas never tasted so good. There is a coconut tree behind my home, a few star fruit trees in the Station area, and I just found a fruit tree a little beyond the coconut tree, full of dozens of baseball size green fruit that taste like sour oranges until they ripen more. There are also plenty of banana trees, papayas, and mangos. The tricky part with them is navigating the "ownership" factor. Each tree is technically "owned" by the missionary who lives closest to them. In other words, I just can't go out and pick what I want.

I haven't figured out the system of asking for some without risking offending somebody, but I'm guessing it's a combination of bartering and generosity.

The same organic freshness is true for the meat sold in town. The fresh meat is mostly local chicken and small fish caught from the river. There is also beef and mystery meat, which is usually goat or sheep — at least that's what they tell us. It could just as easily be monkey, gazelle, or a less savory species. These are sold either frozen or hot after being deliciously slow-grilled by a street vendor. While the grilled chicken is delicious, my favorite meat by far has been gazelle!

I'm confident my foodie friends would have already figured recipes to make the scarce, locally-available fresh foods into beautiful meals. I'm working on discovering how to do so and, frankly, I'm more than a little frustrated by the health risks coupled with the apparent lack of variety. Is it me or is it the remoteness of our location? The jury is still out on whether there are more safe-to-eat fresh foods available. I'm not giving up or giving in to eating exclusively American. After all, I'm in Africa for goodness sake!

I Skyped with my parents on Saturday and told Mom, so I guess I can admit this to the rest of the world: I really miss fresh vegetables and salads! I guess I was eating more healthily back home than I thought. The bottom line is that this whole thing about eating is an incredibly First World problem. I only have to see or smell the cook fires all around the hospital and in the villages to remind me of that. I'm so grateful for my modern, adequately equipped kitchen, good overall diet, and multi-vitamins.

Lessons Learned So Far

1. It's important to ask for advice and recommendations from

people with more experience than I, especially when I'm somewhere new. I'd heard about the potential for limited food options because I had asked lots of questions before I left the States. The bottom line is I'm well-fed and brought over a fantastic multi-vitamin that fills in the nutritional gaps.

2. I can never have enough gratitude. I'm grateful for my modern kitchen and take-out meals from some local restaurants.

3. I'm also grateful that I've learned to think and make up my own mind about things. I'm convinced there are healthy African dishes I just haven't discovered yet. Thanks again, Mom and Dad, for that liberal arts education that taught me to think. There is always another option if I'll only take my time to work it out.

4. Smart, intelligent risks often pay off. So far, I've not gotten food poisoning or worse from what I've eaten or drunk. I'm going to continue to push the envelope in a hopefully smart, safe way.

5. I'm really looking forward to ice cream and chocolate when I get home.

To Ponder

What role do food and nutrition play in my life?

Affirmation

No matter where I am, I eat in a healthy manner!

Eye Exams at School

When I was eight years old in elementary school, we were seated alphabetically. As an "S" last name, it fell on me and my ilk to sit in the back of the classroom. It didn't really matter to me where I sat; I liked school and learning. One day, I was called to read what was on the blackboard. I tried and tried, but I couldn't. I didn't understand. I could read at least one or two grades above third grade level and always got good results on my report card. The teacher, bless her, must have figured out that I needed glasses, because she called me to the front of the room and I was able to easily read whatever the assignment was. I remember being mortified and bursting out in tears, first because I couldn't read and was laughed at by my peers. The second reason was the realization that I needed glasses and the endless teasing and name calling that would come with them. Back then, glasses were *not* fashion symbols, to say the least!

I found myself reliving those moments as I stood against a concrete wall to the side of a classroom at École Privée Nibatoga, the local K-12 school, observing the first school eye screening to ever take place in southern Gabon. Its origins are as a Christian school started long ago by C&MA missionary teachers. Today, it is an interesting blend of government support with Christian teaching in addition to the regular subjects. The school is in the nearby village of Dakar, less than a mile from Bongolo Hospital. Interestingly, the school is a semi-circular sprawl of individual classroom buildings facing a play field rather than a single large building like in the States.

When we drove up to this particular 15-by-20-foot rectangular, single-story classroom, I had the same mix of wonder and sadness I often did the first time I looked at buildings here. This was a typical concrete block building with large, unscreened windows and a corrugated tin roof. The yellow paint has long since faded. The doorway and windows provided for decent air movement. They have no glass or screens, but the windows have stacked horizontal louvers – nockos – to protect against bad rain storms. There must have been some extra money to spend on details. The wooden double doors had locks, but didn't look like they'd been closed in years. Birds, a lot like American barn swallows, swooped in and out through the door and windows, roosters crowed just outside the back windows, and there was an old fluorescent light in the ceiling with no bulb. An aged, room-sized blackboard filled the wall at the front of the class. Students sat at old wooden desks. It was, not surprisingly, a sunny, very hot, and humid morning. They paid absolutely no attention to the heat, roosters, or barn swallows.

This particular class was 26 nine to eleven year olds – middle school kids. All of them were slender and attractive, excited and curious about why we were there. The boy's clothing ranged from jeans and t-shirts to green and white uniforms; the girls almost exclusively wore pretty dresses or skirts (as they get older, jeans and tights begin to appear). The kids struck me as typical 9 to 11 year olds: lively, full of life, and excited at this break in their routine. Their teacher had just introduced Dr. Elisée Makpabo – pronounced "Elleesay" – and nurse Jean Paul from Bongolo Hospital's ophthalmology department. Dr. Elisee explained (in French, of course) that they were there to conduct an eye exam on each of the students. What he didn't tell them was, in fact, they were spending the next week doing eye screenings for all 300 or so kindergarten through senior high students. For an American, this sounds pretty normal.

An eye exam in Gabon, however, needed to be explained, not just to this class but to every class regardless of ages. That's because this was the first time in the *history* of southern Gabon that kids had ever had their vision checked! Why now? The doctors brought with them a cutting-edge screening camera donated for the duration of my trip by the American company, WelchAllyn. Jeff Sommerville in Orchard Park, New York, is a church friend of my parents and he became convicted by the Holy Spirit when he heard about my trip to Bongolo. He launched an urgent, time-crunched crusade to secure one of these "Spot Cameras." God must have really wanted a Spot Camera in Gabon because of the amazing events that led up to the camera arriving at my front door at 7:30 in the morning the day I left, barely two hours before leaving my house for Pittsburgh International Airport!

Spot Camera technology enables anyone with steady hands to take a photograph of a person's eyes. Nearly instantly, an eye glass prescription is displayed on the screen, including astigmatism, if any. A results report can either be printed or transmitted to a computer. From there, a referral is made to an eye professional, if need be. This initial screening methodology is used in schools and community vision screenings across America. Nothing like this has ever been available in southern Gabon and perhaps the entire country. In other words, none of these kids and likely none of their parents, had *ever* been tested to see whether or not they need glasses. That's unbelievable.

Each student went through a double screening. After having their names and ages written in the log book (ironically, in a school notebook with a picture of the Golden Gate Bridge on the cover), they were instructed to stand against the wall at the back of the class and told to cover one eye. Then, Dr. Elisée pointed to a series of letters on a standard eye exam board he had hung on the blackboard. The students would read as much as they could, some confidently and quickly, others slowly and shyly. In this particular class, I was thrilled there was no laughing at anybody who did poorly. The next step was for the student to walk to the front corner of the classroom and Nurse Jean Paul took their eye picture with the Spot Camera. Then, the student returned to his or her seat. Both men would write their results in the log book as a cross check against each method. Testing the entire class took just over an hour.

Of the 88 total students screened in the first two days, 11 were identified as needing a follow up exam, which will be provided free of charge at the Hospital. Invitation notes will be sent home by their teachers soon. I pray these initial 11 and the others of the remaining 200 or so kids will take advantage of this possibly once-in-a-lifetime opportunity to see better.

As much as I hated wearing glasses, the difference they made in my life is dramatic, even today. While standing against that African wall, sweating through my clothes, listening to the roosters and glancing at the barn swallows, I couldn't help but pray that many of these young lives would be different moving forward – simply because they would be able to see much better.

Lessons Learned So Far

1. Teachers care deeply for their students, even at primitive Nibatogo.

2. Kids are kids: goofy, serious, engaged, bored, etc.

3. The compassion I felt for the kids who struggled to read the letters on the blackboard was nearly overwhelming. I wanted to stop the exam and tell my story, but I held back.

4. Many things that at first appear to be big negatives, like glasses on an eight-year-old boy many years ago, are actually blessings in the long run.

To Ponder

What comes to mind when I think about my ability to see?

Affirmation

I utilize every tool (such as glasses) at my disposal to succeed!

Observations & Experiences Part 1

It's been a while since I shared random observations and experiences, so I thought I'd take time to share these with you:

- Giving is an amazing experience. Many of my friends and family donated movies, puzzles, games, and food items that our team brought over. It was an honor to give these basic items to entertainment-hungry people.

- Our team transported a surprise plastic crate on behalf of one of the surgeon's sending church. I had the privilege of being there as it was presented to her. The surprise was complete and I thought she was going to cry.

- We have WiFi through a satellite-based system. The technology is pre-3G and there are around 75 devices vying for the limited Internet access. Faster service is available, but at five times the current cost, which is beyond our resources today. Because of the bandwidth limitations, nobody can stream music or view online videos of any type.

- "No See-Um" bugs, called *bifudo* are real and bite like mosquitos even though they are the size of a coffee ground. Their bites produce a red dot with a pink circular area around it. If I can avoid scratching them, they're pretty much gone in 24 hours.

- Mosquito bites are nearly identical to back home.

- Not scratching is difficult!

- 100% DEET bug spray works well when it's applied correctly.

- Lower DEET concentrations do well but don't last as long.

- *Au de bug* spray is the most popular cologne among us missionaries! Suntan lotion is second.

- All of the plastic bags used by stores are bio-degradable! Apparently it's been the law here and in Europe for years.

- Closets have always-on, low-watt light bulbs because it's so humid that clothes become moldy when hung in a closet or folded in (closed) drawers.

- The bug noises at night sound a lot like summer frogs, cicadas, and crickets.

- There's a bird at dawn that sounds like a black cap chickadee. I love being awakened by singing birds.

- The little white egret birds seem to be the last ones up in the morning (7ish). They remind me of seagulls.

- Chickens are the most common animal at the hospital. The other day, one jumped out from behind a post right in front of me as I was walking past it. Startled, I barely avoided reacting, but I jumped on the inside!

Lessons Learned So Far

1. Curiosity makes seemingly ordinary things come to life.

2. It's fun to observe life around me and attempt to draw conclusions.

3. At times, it's better to just shrug my shoulders than to try to figure things out.

To Ponder

How can I increase my level of curiosity?

Affirmation

My days pass more quickly
when I'm engaged in life around me!

Muslim-Christian Teamwork

For the last seven years, Paul Davis, Director of Maintenance at Bongolo Hospital, has patiently built a relationship with the largest general contractor in the area, Bakary Konate ("Bahk-ah-ree Kone-ah-tay"). Paul is in his early 60s and is in charge of the maintenance and building projects at Bongolo. Bakary is in his early 40s. He is from the country of Mali, but has lived in Gabon most of his life. He's also one of the most prominent Muslim businessmen who dominate the commercial life in the area.

I liked Bakary from the first time I met him. He is a charismatic extrovert and quite entrepreneurial. His primary business is construction, but he also owns at least two food/variety shops and a dozen rental houses. He has by far the nicest African home I've seen (from the outside anyway) since arriving at Bongolo. Paul related how the relationship has grown and changed over the last seven years they've worked together. It's not been easy, particularly at the beginning. Paul speaks enough French to get by, but is by no means fluent; Bakary speaks hardly any English at all.

From the start, Paul appropriately demanded quality construction and made it clear that local African building standards weren't up to his expectations. There have been mighty battles over the years that have always resolved themselves, and led to more work together. Many times, Paul has enlisted the prestigious translation help of Pastor Serge, the Hospital Director to work things out. Paul has worked hard to rein in Bakary's pushy enthusiasm, and to bridge the cultural gaps. Today, there is an obvious mutual business trust and respect between the two. I wouldn't call it friendship — yet.

The first thing the other morning, Paul and I were driving through the Hospital when we stopped to talk with

Bakary about the next steps of the two-month-old construction project of the eye surgery clinic. Bongolo's Ophthalmology Department does nearly every cataract surgery in Gabon as well as other procedures, and patients commonly drive for up to ten hours to come for eye care. It's an understatement that they have more than outgrown their current capacity, and the completion of this two-year project will position Bongolo to help even more people.

After greetings were exchanged, Bakary quickly pulled out his cell phone to show us photos of a truck precariously stuck at a steep angle in one of Africa's great dirt road ditches, with one wheel off the ground. While I didn't know it at the time, it turned out it was Bakary's canvas-covered food delivery truck and this accident had happened the day before, totally blocking the main road about 20 minutes away. They had been bringing in a full load of rolled manioc and large bags of other foodstuffs. AAA and rescue road equipment are non-existent, so the truck sat there all day and throughout the night.

After showing the photos, Bakary quietly asked Paul something, but it was different than usual, and quickly caught my attention. Normally, whenever Bakary asks Paul for any-thing he wants or needs, it's with a wide smile, an offered handshake and an assumptive confidence that communicates he fully expects Paul to say "Yes" to whatever it is. Paul has him figured out, however, and nearly always gives him a loud, hard time. And Bakary is ready for the sparring! Part of it is in fun – guy humor at its best; part is two dominant men vying for power. It's a delicate balance: Bongolo is by far Bakary's largest client, and Bakary is likely the only contractor in the area capable of doing the work we need. Interestingly, it ap-pears that both men understand this.

Not this time. This time, Bakary was quietly respectful and Paul seriously listened, nodded and just as softly said some-thing back. Bakary nodded and we went our separate ways. I'd understood enough to ask Paul if we were going to help, but not enough to really get the whole picture. He nodded yes, and explained about the truck. He predicted it would take us about an hour to go help him out. I immediately understood that this was to be a personal favor and not work related at all.

We quickly finished what we were doing and headed to the garage for the backhoe (*tractor pelle* in French), the only vehicle around big enough to help. A few minutes later, we were on the road to Lébamba. I was sitting in my regular place slightly behind and to the left of Paul, perched on the outside ledge. I held on hard with both hands and my legs braced, anticipating when to lift myself off my hard seat for the spine-jolting impact of each rut and dip in the dirt roads. What a workout! Bakary soon caught up to us with a truck full of his workers, and led us the rest of the way.

A slow, extremely bouncy 20 minutes later, we came upon the truck. The scene was a lot more dramatic than the photos could possibly describe. The zigzagging ruts were among the largest I'd yet seen. And man, was that truck stuck. The front of the truck was facing downhill coming toward us and the rear driver side of the truck was deep in a giant ditch, precariously tipped so that the right front tire was about a foot or more off the ground. It appeared that if it moved much, the truck was going to tip the rest of the way onto its side. Paul looked over at me and dryly said, "I think this is going to take us longer than an hour" and he chuckled.

The story emerged that while the driver was coming down the hill, he attempted to straddle two huge ruts. Unfortunately, the weight of the truck caused the left edge to cave in and his left-rear tire slid into a five-foot-deep dirt drainage gutter. The rear axle and main drive shaft were solidly impeded by the road's rock-hard clay dirt and gravel. That truck wasn't going anywhere without a lot of hard, yet delicate work, otherwise it would roll onto its side. Interestingly, the creative local drivers had long since started a new "road" by driving around the accident through the tall grasses. After all, life goes on even though the road is blocked.

Even though we were a couple of miles outside of Lébamba in the middle of nowhere, there were about 20 men of all ages and sizes waving their arms and giving loud orders, in French, Nzebi, and likely a Malian language, on how the truck should be freed. It was very chaotic! In the States, I would describe them as vocal know-it-alls, backseat drivers, and Monday morning quarterbacks. Interestingly, there were only two shovels and one pick between the lot of them, and Bakary and his men had brought them. The other interesting thing was at least half were dressed in traditional African Islamic garb. Paul and Bakary crawled all around the truck, came up with a plan, and we started to dig.

Thus began a four-hour adventure of modern technology and African muscle teamwork. First, we filled in the gigantic rut in the middle of the road with boulders and dirt dug that were packed down by the backhoe. This was to give the truck a more solid way down the rest of the hill once freed. After that, Paul positioned the *tractor pelle* next to the right side of the truck to attempt to pull the truck out of the ditch, but it proved to be far too heavy for the backhoe. In addition, we believed the truck would tip over completely onto its side if we did so. The strategy was to begin digging out the high portion of the road keeping the truck on three wheels. You should have seen the dance between backhoe and the men with picks and shovels as the truck slowly settled back down onto four wheels.

As the men were digging out underneath the truck, Paul and I went off-road to the left side of the truck. We plowed a path through five-foot high grasses and carefully caved in the embankment next to the truck to give the stuck rear wheel some traction when the time came. The whole time, the peanut gallery was still yelling to pick up the truck! One man in particular came right up to the *tractor pelle* yelling and waving his arms. He looked like he thought he was important. Paul yelled back in French asking if he was going to pay for the damage to the backhoe. Paul just muttered, shook his head, and kept on cutting out the embankment.

Around the time he finished this step, another large delivery truck arrived (Bakary must have called them). It was time for the final stage: get the truck out. So Paul attached the chains again in an effort to pull the truck sideways onto the road while the other truck attempted to pull straight ahead. It worked the first time! The two trucks rumbled over the newly filled in ruts to the safety of flat road, and cheers broke out! Paul parked the backhoe and we got out, shook hands, cheered and slapped backs all the way around. He was the hero!

As we were getting set to leave, Bakary offered to pay Paul, who of course declined. So Bakary instead asked us to stop by his store in Lébamba on the way to get something to drink. We accepted, of course. Paul got a water and I picked out an orange juice. On the way out, Bakary silently lifted a case of each into the *tractor pelle* – a very kind gesture. On the drive back to Bongolo, Paul commented that he wondered if Bakary understood that this was *not* a work-related request to be paid for, but that it was a friend helping a friend. We couldn't tell for sure. The next morning, Paul had the chance to make his point to Bakary through the fluent French translation of Pastor Serge. We think Bakary understood.

Will Paul, Pastor Serge, and the rest of us influence Bakary regarding Christianity? We certainly hope so. Even after seven years, however, it's still relatively early in that journey. A lot of foundation has been laid, but the rest of the relationship still needs to be built. This particular step in the journey was an invigorating and rewarding experience that certainly moved the process forward.

Lessons Learned So Far

1. People are people no matter where in the world I am.

2. Helping a friend is a great way to show Jesus' love.

3. Other religious beliefs are important to recognize and respect if I want to become friends with someone of a different religion. It doesn't mean I have to agree.

4. Love helps friendships develop in spite of conflicting beliefs.

5. At times, it is valuable to utilize another's ability to communicate something important.

To Ponder

Who in my world can I befriend
who doesn't believe what I do?

Affirmation

God uses me to build friendships
for sharing life together!

Life-Saving Blood

Some days are ordinary; some are extraordinary. Today was both. Up until lunch, work was pretty typical except for the sad news of the passing of Olivier's sick sister. Olivier is Paul's right hand man. With heavy hearts, we wished him well as he immediately left work. As is usually the case with this kind of news, off and on throughout the day I pondered the sudden shortness of life and how I might live my life differently. I was again frustrated by my inability to communicate with the men in French and could not pose, let alone understand, the questions about the impact of her death on them that I was burning to ask.

After lunch, Paul, 13-year-old Luke Thelander (who spends every Thursday afternoon with Paul), Joures, Antoine, and I took the dump truck and backhoe to the hospital's main square to spend the afternoon clearing away rubble and construction debris from the progressing building project: the newly, renovated, and expanded areas for outpatient care and for maternity patients. My part of the project was to wait for the backhoe to fill up the dump truck, then drive it the quarter mile to the dumping area and come back.

At about three o'clock, it rained quite hard for an hour or so. Our work became wet; puddles and brick red mud were everywhere. We were all muddy and wet. At one point, I grew tired of sitting while I waited for the next load, so I jumped out into a muddy puddle and walked over to stand underneath the roof of the emergency room building. I was lost in thought when I heard a voice at my elbow. It was the maternity director, Dr. Elizabeth Elliott — Izzi to us, Dr. Izzi to her patients. Izzi is, I'm guessing, in her early thirties and is a woman of great faith, passion, and focus. She is rapidly becoming a leader here after arriving just two years ago. We hadn't really talked much, so I was a little surprised when she walked up next to me.

"Have I ever asked you what your blood type is?" was not how I expected her to start the conversation. I said, "Hi, Izzi" and smiled. I assured her that she hadn't, then told her it was O-something. "What's going on?" Her reply stunned me. In essence, she said, "Will you donate blood right now to save the life of a young late-stage pregnant woman with severe sickle cell anemia (note: this is a common hereditary disease in Africa)? She and her unborn child will both die if they don't receive a transfusion and I do an emergency Caesarian section to get the baby out. Frankly, I don't know how the mom has lived this long." There was no 'likely' or 'might' would die. I immediately said "Yes," and she started me walking toward the lab. "Wait, right *now*?" I asked. She nodded curtly and replied, "Right now."

I asked her to hold on a second. First, I explained that, no matter how much I wanted to donate blood in the States, I am not allowed to because I lived in England 35 years ago (Mad Cow disease had been an issue in the 1980s). She gave a little smile and replied that my blood is perfectly fine for Africa. Then, I excused myself and ran over to Paul in the backhoe to briefly explain what I was going to do, and arranged for Antoine to take my place in the dump truck. Then, we were off to the lab, a muddy, couple-of-minutes-walk away. I asked her why she just didn't get blood from the blood bank, and she answered that Bongolo isn't equipped to store blood and that the blood bank is walking around. That was amazing to me; I'd never before considered that a hospital wouldn't have a supply of blood on hand (besides nearby people).

Once there, I greeted my friend, Siko, who runs the lab. I had the pleasure of being Siko's guest for church and for dinner and very much enjoyed him and his wife, Delphine. I think this surprised Izzi, but she covered well. She then introduced me to a couple of other African technicians, then asked me if I was comfortable being left with them. I replied I was and asked her how soon the Caesarean would take place. "As soon as they draw your blood and I can pump it into her" was the answer.

The first step was to take a small blood sample to check the type and to test for AIDS and hepatitis. It wasn't as straightforward as that because the techs only spoke French. They got their points across well enough for us to get through the process. Of course, this being remote Africa, the power went out part way through the testing and, amid mass groaning, the testing needed to be restarted a few seconds later once the generator kicked in, thus losing precious minutes. About 10 minutes after that, I received a thumbs-up report and they walked me to the nearby padded table to draw the blood.

They inserted the needle and my blood began to flow into a bag. At about that time, Izzi returned, looking stressed even though she was hiding it well. Lying there, I couldn't help myself, so I asked her if we get cookies and Gatorade when the technicians were done. She laughed (my whole point) and just shook her head. While she was waiting for my blood, I asked her if I could observe the operation. That sudden, Holy Spirit-inspired idea seemed like the most natural request I could make. After all, I reasoned, now I had skin in the game! This startled her a little bit, but she quickly recovered and said I could.

Another 10 or so minutes went by and Izzi, after answering some more questions about the mom (very young, first baby) and the nature of sickle cell anemia, surprised me by personally taking possession of the unit of my blood and headed across campus to the operating room. Fortunately, the rain had stopped. After resting for a couple minutes and assuring the lab techs I wasn't going to pass out, I followed in her wake up to the OR building. As I entered, I couldn't believe my eyes: I saw Izzi personally walking the mom into the operating room, holding aloft the bag of my blood as it seeped into her arm. I choked up.

She came back out in a minute and handed me a hair wrap and a surgical mask to tie on. That was it. I showed her my muddy boots and dirty, wet clothes, but she said they were all right. That wouldn't be the case back home, that's for sure! She took me into the OR and, with the mom laying there, explained that a nurse would take the newborn baby to an incubator in the maternity building after he/she was born. I asked if it would be permissible to take non-invasive photos, and she turned to the woman and asked in French for her permission, which was granted. My last question was concerning the best place for me to stand out of the way. Izzi pointed to the corner and instructed me to stand there. Again, I couldn't help myself and replied that's the most natural place in the world for me. A quick smile was all I got this time and she turned to the task at hand. The young woman was bathed and prepped for surgery, including an epidural anesthesia.

Just before the first incision, Izzi paused, looked up at me, and asked me if I'd pray. I was surprised. I knew this was part of every surgery and consultation, but as the lead surgeon, I expected Izzi to do this. "I'd be honored to," was my reply. After about 30 seconds of asking for God's provision and guidance, the operation began.

Two other things happened during the procedure that caught me off guard. The first was when my friend Dr. Simplice, one of the African surgeons, popped his head in. He looked surprised to see me standing there and asked if I'd ever seen a surgery before. I told him no, and that I'd just given blood for this procedure. "Would you like a stool?" he asked, suddenly looking very doctor-like and said, "I'll be right back." He brought it right in like it was a totally normal thing to do. He was another surgeon doing minor tasks in the name of service. This was contrary to my idea of doctors in general and surgeons specifically.

At some point shortly after this, I noticed the rumble of the backhoe as Paul and Antoine kept working on the other side of the building. It's easy to denigrate maintenance and construction, but it – my work – is also important work. Thankfully, I knew this already, but the significance of what some might consider menial work blended in beautifully to what Izzi and Simplice had so naturally done to help another person as part of their day.

The other thing that surprised me was that the mom was awake and responsive during the 45-minute operation. It had been so long since I had stood in two other delivery rooms during my own children's births that I forgot that consciousness is one of the benefits of an epidural. A couple of times early in the operation before her baby was born, the mom looked over at me as I stood quietly in the corner. It caught me off guard at first, but I felt God's presence around me and her, and I smiled to her as confidently and reassuringly as I could, and each time her eyes lit up with gratitude, which blew me away. A little bit later, Izzi happily announced, "*C'est une fille!*" It's a girl!

When the baby was safely delivered, the deep emotions I'd kept just below the surface burst out in silent tears of joy. *Thank You, God!* was how I began. *Thank You for orchestrating the entire afternoon. Thank You for my good health and blood type. Thank You for Western medical care available right here, in the middle of the jungle. Thank You that the mom and baby did so well in the face of high odds of either or both dying.* My list went on and on.

About 90 minutes after Izzy's request to give blood, I wandered out to the courtyard to watch Paul finish clearing and leveling the square, enjoying being alone for a few minutes. Bakary, the Muslim general contractor, was there too, killing time at the end of his day, and he and couple of his men wandered over. After the normal greetings, I quickly decided to build on the helping theme from the other day, and shared everything I could in my limited French about my experience just now, including my gratitude for God's provision. I showed him pictures of the baby being born, and the fresh scab on the inside of my elbow. It took lots of gestures and frequent typing into my Google Translate, but he got it, and also thanked God. It was a cool and totally unexpected 30 minutes together to share God's love with another person.

As Paul worked and Antoine took load after load away, I marveled at the simple way I had contributed to life at Bongolo Hospital. All I had done was give blood, something I've wanted to do for years back home, but could not. My action was nothing more than a simple, "Yes" to a prompting, but it made all the difference today to a young mom and her baby. I'm humbled to have been used this way, and grateful to have been here in Africa to help out.

Postscript: Both the mom, Amanda, and baby Naomi have done well, and I took the opportunity to visit them before I left. Izzi translated and she took a beautiful photo of the three of us. Naomi will be at the hospital in an incubator for another month at least. What a heart-warming way to wrap up an amazing experience!

Lessons Learned So Far

1. There is no such thing as menial work. All work has value in the kingdom of God.

2. The most surprising people will do "menial work" and think nothing of it. Izzi didn't hesitate to ask me personally to donate blood, and she took it upon herself to wait for it and to personally walk my unit of blood to the operating room. Also, Simplice didn't delegate getting me a stool.

He did it personally with a big, warm smile. Not many physicians, let alone surgeons, would have done either.

3. Smiling to reassure a total stranger in need is a great way to show Jesus' love. It also filled me with warmth and joy, a wonderful side benefit!

4. I understood the "saving blood of Christ" in a whole new way today, in a completely *human* way. Because I was asked to help, my blood helped save two peoples' lives. Jesus, in a totally *God* way, saves us from our sins, just by us asking.

To Ponder

How will I respond to a possibly surprise request for help?

Affirmation

In a healthy way, it is natural for me to say "yes" to most requests for help!

A Quick History

Investigating and learning the history of a place is far more interesting as one prepares to travel there, or when already there. Both have certainly been true of my trip to Bongolo. Prior to departure, I had read just one background book: *On Call*, the autobiography of Bongolo's founder, Dr. David Thompson. Since being here, I've read two additional Bongolo-related books, one the biography of the first missionary, Donald Fairley, called *Beyond the Mist*; the other was *His Hand on My Scalpel*, which is a collection of Bongolo stories from a surgeon's perspective. Both of these works were also written by David Thompson. He was also the driving force behind the historical DVD, also called *Beyond The Mist*, an interesting, hour-long video about Bongolo's founding and early days. Since arriving here, I can't get enough information about this fascinating, God-filled place. Let me share the following highlights of what I have learned.

Bongolo Hospital has operated since 1977 when the first missionary surgeon, Dr. David Thompson, arrived with his wife, three nurses and a small support staff. David's sending church was ACAC (my church home in Pittsburgh). This explains why my church is such a big fan of Bongolo. It's amazing what David and his team built from a tiny medical dispensary in the middle of the jungle, far from "civilization." Today, the sprawling campus and missionary homes cover the three plateaus above the river. The doctors, residents and other missionaries live on the top two levels, a steep quarter mile above the hospital itself.

Forty-three years of amazing missionary work in Gabon preceded this medical miracle in the jungle. In the early 1930s, California animal trainer Don Fairley and his wife were a normal American couple, living a respectable and comfortable life. That is until they heard and responded to the plea for people to go to Central Africa to bring Christ to a people who had never heard the Good News of the Creator God or Jesus Christ. Like many in Central Africa then and today, they worshipped their ancestors, feared demons, and participated in medicine-man-led ceremonial cannibalism. The Fairley's went through a long period of preparation, consisting of language school in France, as French was (and still is) the official language, then a period of time in mission-based evangelical and theology training, first in Gabon, then back in the United States.

The northern part of Gabon and the surrounding lands that were soon to become independent countries, had been well-seeded by missionaries. No one, however, had ever penetrated into southern Gabon, "the white man's graveyard" as it was known. They were a totally unreached people group of disparate tribes and languages, including several pigmy villages. Don was captivated by this potential, and his first trip to southern Gabon was in early 1933, when he and a team set out from the mission headquarters town of Lambaréné, in central Gabon, the same town where Dr. Albert Schweitzer had founded his now famous hospital 20 years earlier.

The purpose of Don's trip was to locate a site somewhere in southern Gabon where a long-term mission might be established. Since there were no roads (paved roads outside of cities and large towns are a recent development in Gabon), they surveyed the hundreds of miles by motorized river barge, canoe, and on foot.

At one point, they camped for an extended period of time at the base of Bongolo Falls, about 150 miles south and east of Lambaréné, a geographical touch-point for seven tribes. Fairley immediately saw the potential for a mission base there. In addition to being warmly received by the native Africans, he envisioned a future hydro-electric plant. He made arrangements with the local chiefs to purchase the land, then to return as soon as possible to live there. He and his team headed back for Lambaréné to report in and to plan.

Two years later, along with several other missionaries, Don and his wife, Dorothy, returned for their first multi-year assignment to the people around Bongolo Falls. After enlisting the aid of hundreds of laborers, building began. They started with pole and thatch houses similar to the ones in the villages; eventually, they began to build using home-made bricks and mortar. The amount of manual labor time needed for these projects is astounding by today's standards! Years would go by before construction of a home could even begin. Just the act of clearing the jungle trees and grasses took months, let alone digging out the hillsides to level the land, plus accumulating and making by hand the huge quantities of hand-cut wood boards and brick materials.

Right from the start, the construction workers heard the gospel message and many became Christians. The new Christ followers enrolled in Bible school studies and several would go on to become local evangelists, pastors, as well as regional and national leaders. Today, tribal spirit worship still exists in some places, and Islam has made inroads, but Christianity, more than 82 years since Don Fairley's first survey trip, has become the dominant religion in southern Gabon. Just last year, 2,200 souls from Bongolo Hospital alone welcomed our Savior, Jesus Christ, into their hearts.

Lessons Learned So Far

1. Visionary people can be intimidating and almost scary when looked at in hindsight. The obstacles the Fairleys and others overcame are mind boggling in light of today's technology and conveniences. They seem super human to me.

2. Visionary people put their pants on one leg at a time, however, just like I do. They go to work in their called area and do the best they can. I do, too!

3. Many of their amazing accomplishments were simply the necessary next steps in a progression of meeting needs and solving problems.

4. Who knows, history may very well look back on my/your work and call us visionaries! Wouldn't that be something?

To Ponder

What am I beginning (or building upon)
that will help future generations?

Affirmation

I build for the future!

What an Adventure!

A number of people predicted I would be a different person by the time I get home. They think it will be obvious to me and to others. I have to admit, I don't know what to think about that prediction. While I'm already aware of some changes, it's more likely that I'm changing but can't sense it. For example, I'm aware of a couple of small things. One is I can't even begin to convey how much I'm *loving* that my cell phone volume is "off" all the time (because I'm halfway around the world), as well as to not be as crazily busy while still working very hard. My life here feels like it's more focused, perhaps because this is a somewhat less complicated place.

Maybe these changes people are anticipating will be similar to when I came home after being a high school senior exchange student for a year. I lived with a great family north of Manchester, England and had a wonderful, life-changing experience. The day I left England to come home, my English friends were still calling me "Yank" and taking the mickey (teasing me) about my American accent. I was convinced nothing about me had changed. Somehow, on the airplane back to Buffalo, NY, I developed this really thick English accent! Nobody said anything, so the first time I became aware of this was after I'd reclaimed my job as a lifeguard at the village pool. The first time I blew my whistle at a kid for something, I yelled, "Oy, you! Come 'ere." Everybody in the pool stopped and looked at me!

The *Merriam-Webster Dictionary* defines adventure as: "1: an undertaking usually involving danger and unknown risks; 2: an exciting or remarkable experience." Every time I consider the subject of adventure, I'm reminded of a scene from the sequel to *Jurassic Park* when a couple of kids were talking about how much they would like to go on an adventure and are overheard by Ian Malcolm (Jeff Goldblum), who survived the first movie. He says something to them along the lines of, "Hey, kid! You want to know what an adventure is? It's a lot of running and screaming, and living to tell about it."

Of course, that's an extreme description. My more mundane perspective is that every day can become an adventure or have a component of adventure, even when nothing dramatic happens. Regardless of what we do at work, out and about, or at home, we can all choose to live in the perspective that there are interesting, new, fun, silly, and exciting aspects to every day, if we will just pay attention. Each one is an opportunity to express gratitude to God and to learn something. After nearly a month and a half at Bongolo, there hasn't been any screaming, but there have been adventures galore. Here are just a few:

- The flight from Paris to Libreville had a loud, restrained prisoner who was being extradited back to Gabon. I was approached by a policeman as I entered my part of the plane and he did his best to explain the situation.

- When I saw a major Third World city (Libreville) for the first time and was stunned by the poverty and primitive conditions.

- Riding shotgun in a Cessna airplane for the two-hour flight to Bongolo over uninhabited jungle. Rising above and descending below clouds will never be the same.

- Once at Bongolo, our first visit to the new eye center construction site was an 'eye opener,' to say the least. I experienced terror as I watched the other three men "tight rope walking" on four-inch beams, 20 feet above ground, like it was nothing. I like heights, but have battled a fear of falling off high things for years, so I cringed and silently screamed in fear on the inside. In my imagination, they fell a hundred times before we even started work.

- Day one on the job site, I needed to cross a four-foot section of exposed beam to step onto the 20-foot-high second floor mentioned in the prior point. I did, but doing so scared me for days. I eventually got quite comfortable.

- When I saw a fluorescent green snake in the root bowl of a giant kapok tree and dashed backwards the ten feet to the road faster than I thought I could move. All snakes in Gabon are poisonous and brightly colored ones are nature's way of warning others away.

- We're always to have flashlights at night as we've been told snakes often come out after dark. Sayings like "a snake in the grass" and "it's a good thing you're not a poisonous snake" have taken on entirely new meanings.

- The first time at church where it's two-and-a-half hours in French and I stick out like a sore thumb because of my whiteness.

- Feeling really exposed and intimidated the first time we went food shopping in Lébamba. Talk about culture shock! Now, I feel quite comfortable.

- Attempting to speak French when I only know a little bit. The Google Translate app has been a godsend! My interest in communicating has also captured the imaginations of many of the men and women I come into contact with. So far, everyone has been kind and patient with me.

- Driving heavy equipment – every boy's dream come true! I've had the opportunity to work the backhoe and haul things in the dump truck. I want more backhoe time!

- Speaking of driving, I was told I'm a very good jungle driver after successfully and safely negotiating badly rutted dirt roads for the very intense 45 minutes each way to and from worshiping at a village church. There were times I think God sent angels to keep us safe.

- Worshiping in French at a village church while sitting on a hard wooden bench for three hours. I've been to two so far, and experiencing the joy and praise of the same God I worship in the States was really cool.

- Leading eight men who speak less English than I do when Paul Davis was away on vacation or at a four-day team prayer retreat meeting. We got the job done.

- Adjusting to high heat and humidity. It's been a surprise that my body actually seems to like this weather!

- And, of course, the biggest adventure of all was giving emergency blood to save the life of a very sick mom in labor and her premature baby, then standing in the operating room to watch the baby's birth!

Lessons Learned So Far

1. I hope and pray that every day holds at least one adventure, just preferably not the *Jurassic Park* kind.

2. My daily challenge is to recognize adventures when they're happening, to enjoy the ride, and then share the joy of them with the right people.

3. Adventures are great opportunities to express my thanks to the Lord.

To Ponder

What is my perspective on the word "adventure"?

Affirmation

Adventures are how I grow and mature!

Evaluating Daily Routines Part 1

Being away from home for two months has given me the opportunity to evaluate, test, keep, discard, and adopt new daily routines. Where better to do this than in the middle of the jungle, far away from my fast-paced urban lifestyle?

From the start, I knew I would be giving up many aspects of my life and resolved to make my peace with it. The most obvious is giving up First World comforts for an unknown Third World way of life. Some small things are no supermarkets, craft beer, ice cream, pubs to sit and talk with friends, restaurants, or big screen movies. I'd also be giving up normal routines with family, friends, and work and volunteer associates. At first, the only people I would know would be the four brand new friends I would travel, live, eat, and work with for the first two weeks here. Finally, I was giving up speaking English, at least some of the time, as everyone speaks French or a tribal language, and very little to no English.

I also saw this as an opportunity to preserve and improve habits I consider to be critical: daily devotional time, eating well, exercising, and getting enough sleep, to name a few. Therefore, I resolved to conduct an intentional two-month experiment around three questions:

1. What could I eliminate that had been bothering me at home but I never seemed to make any progress?

2. What could I modify and do more of that I like doing or is good for me?

3. What new things would I like to do?

Eliminate watching movies. I chose to focus on one aspect of my American life: watching movies. This will sound silly to some, but my biggest internal struggle over the last few months was related to watching too many movies at night. I choose not to have cable TV or online movies because I have trouble turning them off and going to bed. Instead, I watch DVDs so I can turn them off and start back up again whenever I like. This seemingly harmless routine had begun to take over. It didn't feel like I was in control any longer.

I had allowed the habit of watching some, if not all, of a movie to grow to be part of nearly every evening. I thought I deserved the break after coming home from a long day at work, exercising at the Y, and having many business, volunteer, or social meetings after that. Regardless of how I spun it, it was still rationalizing a habit I didn't like or want any longer.

I'm pleased to report I've watched no movies (except for the documentary history of the founding of the mission here at Bongolo in the 1930s). And you know what? I haven't missed them. I've filled my evenings with more fulfilling activities.

Lessons Learned So Far

1. When I choose to give up something I've been doing, it isn't a loss – it's an opportunity to grow.

2. It's not as difficult to give up a distracting habit as I thought it would be, and I'm glad I had a plan to keep me strong.

3. I'm more peaceful inside since I'm not sitting in front of the movie screen. Also, I've slept better than I have in years.

To Ponder

*What have I been wanting to give up doing,
and how might doing so benefit me?*

Affirmation

It's easy to make changes!

Evaluating Daily Routines Part 2

This two-month "daily routine" experiment has proven to be quite fruitful. I am working through answers to these three questions:

1. What could I eliminate that had been bothering me at home but I never seemed to make any progress?

2. What could I modify and do more of that I like doing or is good for me?

3. What new things would I like to do?

We discussed eliminating movies. Now, let's take a look at the second issue: routines I wanted to modify. These fall into two complementary categories: those that are good for me, and those I enjoy. In my ideal world, the two will intersect all the time, but I'm not there yet. Two important examples of routines that I have modified are exercise and eating.

Working out has been a high priority of mine ever since playing high school and college sports. Exercising is a critical part of staying healthy as I age. That's not to say that I've always worked out the way I want to. But, for a year or so before leaving for Bongolo, 1 had gotten back into a good system of running and taking CrossFit classes at my YMCA. When I arrived at Bongolo in late January, I was in the best shape I'd been in the last couple years. That's not to say I was where I wanted to be. I was still twenty pounds heavier and not as strong as I wanted to be. Not surprisingly, there is no organized gym here in the jungle, so I got creative developing workouts that, while familiar, were also different.

For example, my running became trotting 2-3 days a week up and down steep hills. I've also been going on a long walk on Saturday or Sunday mornings, and have worked up to nearly two hours of intense hill walking. There are two half-marathons in May that I have half an eye on doing if I can be ready. Recently, I started running or walking with Rob Peterson, the pilot, when he goes through the nearby village of Dakar. I'd been advised to stay in the mission because I don't speak French. I have found this to be very restrictive and, while I was initially nervous about accidentally getting into trouble, venturing forth with him has given me the confidence to go to the bridge and back on my own.

As far as my CrossFit classes, I've adapted a few of the body-weight exercises so I can gain strength even though I'm not currently lifting weights. I've found ways to work out here that both provide great physical benefits and utilize the terrain and available items to lift. My favorite is the very old metal swing set like the ones in my elementary school playground. There's a bar to swing on that makes for great modified pull ups. There are also rings, but I've not used them much *yet*.

Of course, working out in the non-air conditioned jungle has the added challenge of high heat and humidity, even at the end of the day. Back home, the peak hot summer days are either days off or they mean a trip to the air conditioned YMCA. Not here; hot and humid is every day, which leaves only two choices: to work out or not. It's really interesting that I've done my best to ignore the elements and press on. Maybe it's simply because I don't have any choice if I'm going to accomplish my personal goals. I've been smart and stayed as hydrated as possible, then I ring out my shirt when I'm done. Overall, I'm doing pretty well with working out; I'm pleased with the weight I've lost so far, and I feel stronger.

The other major routine I've modified is how I eat. As mentioned in an earlier chapter, back home I eat out often and eat leftovers the rest of the time. Cooking is something I do either because I'm out of leftovers, want an omelet, or have a foodie friend over and he or she takes the lead. I'm actually pretty good in the kitchen; I just don't enjoy it as a single man.

My challenge at Bongolo has been to cook more since eating out options are severely limited, which is an understatement to say the least. While I've figured out how to have some takeout meals to the amusement of everyone, the locals use a *lot* of palm oil, which I'm not used to. Therefore, I've spent more time in meal preparation and clean up than at home. The ingredients are limited compared to the States, but I've made do just fine. I think I'm going to continue to cook more once I get back to the States. It's a lot less expensive, I control the ingredients, and it feels more responsible to me than my prior pattern. Maybe I'll also entertain more as an incentive.

Lessons Learned So Far

1. Creatively changing my routines has been more fun than I expected it to be.

2. It's good for me to be forced to make changes. It's caused me to re-examine my attitudes. Cooking is a great example.

3. Getting other people involved produces unexpected benefits. Connecting with Rob regarding running led me to get off the Station. I was free!

4. I've enjoyed having dinner with many people since arriving here. I intend to begin to reciprocate while I'm here, as well as to host small dinners more often at home rather than meet friends out to eat.

To Ponder

How can I modify an existing routine or habit to benefit myself or others?

Affirmation

I'm very creative when I give myself the opportunity!

Evaluating Daily Routines Part 3

Let's wrap up discussing my "daily routines" experiment. I set out to answer three questions and to gauge the impact on my life. What do I want to eliminate?; What do I want to modify?; and What new things would I like to do now? This third question is the fun one! The first two represent changes to things I was doing. Implementing the answers to this third question has made my time here richer and even more fulfilling.

I approached "new things I'd like to do" from a lifestyle-change perspective. I could have also looked at this from an "adventure" perspective, which would have had a list of things I'd like to do so I could enjoy the experience. One-time events, however, are not what this experiment has been about. I wanted to see how making some changes to the way I spend my free time would impact me. Even with daily exercising, evenings with missionary friends, writing, and preparing meals, I've still had plenty of evening and weekend time on my hands. While I could have selected other things, here is my list for now:

✓ write more.

✓ read more.

✓ learn as much French as possible.

✓ complete jigsaw puzzles.

Write more. Before I left Pittsburgh, my friend and mentor, John Stanko, had asked me if I was going to write while I was gone, and I replied I would be blogging about my experiences. He then said that would make a good book for anybody considering a missionary trip and the idea stuck. Instead of writing 15-20 minutes most days, I've been writing, my old average, one to two hours a day, mostly in the evenings. This has produced 28,500 words so far, which blows my mind. That's the equivalent of 114 paperback book pages. I've also kept a small personal journal book of events, impressions, emotions, and ponderings. Who knows when or if that will come in handy!

Read more. At home, I read an average of a book a month. In addition, I have my morning daily quiet time in the Bible – I'm reading through the Bible in two years as part of a program through church. Finally, I read the devotional *My Utmost for His Highest* every day. So far, in addition to the daily Bible and *My Utmost* readings, I've finished nine books – four were fiction and five were non-fiction. The non-fiction books have been about Bongolo and its history, and Dr. Albert Schweitzer, who spent much of his lauded life in Gabon at his famous hospital about four hours north of here. I've also read portions of five others that I intend to finish while I'm here. These are Christian growth books with subjects such as understanding Muslims, deepening my belief in the reliability of the Bible, and growing in surrender to and trust of God. I find them harder reading and have intentionally broken them into chunks.

The fiction books have all been in the Tarzan series. Actually, I read them all in my youth and decided that since many of the stories take place in the Gabon region of central Africa, what better book could I read? After all, I need *some* distraction from being productive!

Play more. My other distraction activity has been to reconnect (pun intended ☺) with my love of jigsaw puzzles. From boyhood into adulthood, it was common for us to have a puzzle out, and Mom, my brother Jeff, and I would spend hours pouring over the hundreds of pieces. Dad would drop in occasionally on his way through the room, but he did not enjoy them like we did. We'd talk, half watch TV, and listen to music. When one was done, it seemed that we always had a next challenge. A fun pattern developed pretty early: Both Jeff and I wanted to be the one to put in the last piece. Eventually, one of us would slip one piece into a pocket and whoever could hold out the longest won that contest. It made for a lot of laughing and finger pointing, especially when the last piece really was missing.

I've not set out a jig-saw puzzle for years, however, due to owning cats. I haven't figured out a way to keep them off the table as they make a play-filled mess. All I could imagine was them jumping up, knocking the pieces all around, then laying down on top of the remaining pieces to watch me. When I had the chance to work on a puzzle here, I jumped at it. By the time I leave, I'm projecting I'll have finished four. The first two, octagonal shaped "Flags of the World" and a round "Birds of North America" were both donated by my folks, and I brought them over to share, never thinking I'd be the first to do them, The third has been a real project: a photograph of the American side of Niagara Falls which I found in the library here. Doing this one was a no-brainer since I grew up less than an hour from the Falls. It has been fun attempting to describe this in French! The fourth will be a mountain lake photo.

The bonus of doing puzzles is that I've listened to music as well as hours of French-phrase audio recordings I brought with me. Both disappear into the background of intense focus, but I know I've picked up more French than I had before in the same way I learned the words to hundreds of songs and commercial jingles through constant repetition. What I haven't done so far and want to do is to invite my new friends over to work on a puzzle together. I'm working on this!

Earlier, I used the phrase "spend my time" to describe my down time back home. It is more accurate to now say, "invest my time," as I have benefitted from these changes as well as thoroughly enjoyed them. I've achieved more consistent peace-of-mind, learned enough French to get by (but still have a million miles to go), and reconnected with a beloved childhood activity that I've missed. Finally, the fact that I've written so many pages astounds me.

My next experiment will be, "How will I answer the same three questions once I get home?" I'm pretty certain one answer will be to find a way to cat-proof a puzzle.

Update: I actually read 18 books while at Bongolo, five fiction and the rest non-fiction. All five fiction works were Tarzan books. Also, I completed the fourth puzzle the day before I left.

Lessons Learned So Far

1. It's incredibly satisfying to resume activities I've loved in the past.

2. Not watching movies has been a gigantic blessing. Instead of feeling deprived, I've felt empowered.

3. I have to guard against getting sucked into a puzzle just like I do a movie. The time passes so quickly and, unless I'm really disciplined, I will say, "Just one more piece" until it's way past my bed time and I'm faced with being too tired the next day.

To Ponder

What do I love to do and have not done for years?

Affirmation

*Filling my time with activities
I love is incredibly satisfying!*

Learning a New Language

"They don't happen to speak Spanish there, do they?" was my plaintive question back in October to Blaine Workman when he first introduced me to the idea of going to Bongolo Hospital. I'd spent several years half-heartedly learning Spanish phrases in anticipation of serving God in South America. My dream idea was to become an itinerant life coach and handyman to missionaries so I could become fluent in Spanish. I had it all planned out and only needed a little help from God. It would have been a good idea to ask Him what He thought of my plan, don't you agree?

Because that was *my* idea, not God's, that plan never went anywhere at all. Everyone I told patiently nodded and smiled as I told my tale. Then, they all went their way, I'm sure forgetting about it as soon as they were gone. It was frustrating that this great idea *of mine* never gained any traction. So, I continued to pick away at learning Spanish phrases as best I could.

Three years passed before Blaine suggested I go to Bongolo. That meant a total shift, however, because French is Gabon's national language, not Spanish. Fortunately for me, both are romantic languages with a common root syntax. After realizing that this time I was in the middle of a God-plan instead of one of my creation, I made a bee-line for the library to check out every French language CD I could get my hands on. I also bought Rosetta Stone language software that I loaded onto my laptop. I was really dedicated for a few weeks, but then I started to sluff off some. I'd still listen to my French audio, but I didn't stick to it. Just before leaving, I got serious again about learning as much as I could, but it just wasn't enough. I boarded the airplane and decided to do my best once I arrived.

The missionaries based at Bongolo (and in other countries) fortunately follow a different path to language acquisition.
They need to be pretty fluent right from the start due to patient
and other responsibilities, in addition to discussing Christian
ideas and beliefs. Furthermore, they are expected to carry on
normal conversations in French. The solution for them is to
spend six to twelve months in a language school in France.
They are totally immersed into life in a French-speaking town,
and they attend long classroom sessions with others at a similar
language level. By the time they arrive at Bongolo, they are at
least conversant if not fluent.

The first week or so at Bongolo, it was really exciting to
try out and perfect the handful of phrases I knew. Amazingly,
greetings and asking how someone is doing really worked.
More importantly, the people I was attempting to communicate with seemed to truly appreciate the fact that I was trying
my best. I thought it was important to pronounce French as
authentically as possible, and I was regularly complimented
on my accent. The problem was I often couldn't remember
what I'd just said, let alone be able to repeat it next time. My
little notebook that I carried everywhere was gradually being
filled with specific French vocabulary. In addition, the Google
Translate phone app was a total lifesaver over and over.

After two or so weeks passed, however, I found myself
increasingly frustrated because I couldn't communicate anything besides polite basics. I went through a period of not
wanting to speak French at all because I was embarrassed that
my little bit of French was so pitiful. I had to speak, but I
didn't want to. I'm curious and love great conversations, and I
was dying to ask all kinds of life and work questions, but was
unable to do so. One of my blessings at that point was when
Sandy Freeman, one of the nursing school instructors, took me
under her wing to give me a few French grammar lessons. It
was great to begin to understand the "why" behind the phrases

I was learning through my own study.

With about three weeks to go, I rededicated myself to learning as much French as possible while there. I found when Paul was away and I ran maintenance that I learned at a much more rapid rate because I wasn't speaking much English during the day. I resolved that, for everyone's benefit if I ever return as a missionary, I will be fluent before my arrival.

Lessons Learned So Far

1. It shows respect to people of a different country to speak at least a little bit of their language, especially when I'm in their country.

2. It's fun to be understood in a foreign tongue. It was fulfilling that the phrases I'd learned worked.

3. It's very lonely when pretty much all you can discuss is how someone is today. My other French was limited to what I needed at work to understand the needs of the eight-man maintenance crew.

4. Frustrated can't begin to describe my emotions when I wanted to have more of a conversation with a non-English speaker.

5. It is embarrassing not to speak French.

To Ponder

*How many ways can I come up with
to learn something that's important to me?*

Affirmation

I assertively step into unfamiliar experiences!

Opposites Attract

What does a leading surgeon talk about with a maintenance guy? In America, not very much and not very often. That's not the case here at Bongolo Hospital. Here, the rules of the informal but real American caste system don't apply. Whether a person is a physician or important support person, everybody works together to fulfill the mission of providing top quality, Christ-centered medical care to the people of Gabon. In my opinion, the best example of this is the deep friendship and working relationship between Dr. Keir Thelander and Paul Thompson. We've met both in prior chapters.

Keir is the charismatic medical director and missionary team leader. He and his young family answered God's call to missionary service ten years ago as a result of an email want ad. Interestingly, prior to medical school, Keir was trained as an electrical engineer. He also has a visionary mindset full of plans and ideas for Bongolo's future, which include building and infrastructure changes and improvements. He is not your typical surgeon by any stretch of the imagination.

Paul, a retired automobile manufacturing maintenance supervisor from Michigan, has served as maintenance director here for seven years. He and his wife, Meladee, had been on annual short-term trips for years and had decided to seek a missionary posting to retire into. God brought them to Bongolo. Paul had spent his career working in the highly automated world of American automobile manufacturing, eventually leading a plant maintenance team of about 25 people. Since his arrival at Bongolo, he has remade the physical infrastructure and built several new hospital and residence buildings. Seven years later, there are fewer and fewer major surprises and issues for his team of eight Gabonese men to contend with.

When you dig a little bit below the surface, you quickly

arrive at a better understanding of how these two men (and their families) have bonded. Both are men of deep Christian faith, surrendered to serving God as He directs. Both are humble experts. The two families have grown closer and closer over the last seven years, and Paul and Meladee have become adopted grandparents to 13-year-old Luke and 11-year-old Sarah.

Whenever there is a nonmedical crisis of any kind, both men are quick to call in the other for a fresh set of eyes. It's a regular occurrence that either Paul will call up Keir when he's stumped, or for Keir to come find Paul to help diagnose an electrical problem at the hospital. They operate under the old Ronald Reagan idea that you can accomplish anything as long as you don't care who gets the credit.

And it's a good thing, because every ounce of that symbiosis was needed when the main generator, the one that runs the entire Hospital and living quarters, went down. It's not an over exaggeration to say that consistent, predictable electricity is the most important non-medical aspect of delivering patient care. It is clearly the most important of our four backup generators. Back home an outage is usually just an inconvenience. Here, it is a matter of life and death. Just imagine if there was no back-up generator (life in Bongolo's not-so-distant past). I shudder at the implications. What if the power goes out in the middle of a sensitive surgery, a premature baby can't stay warm in his/her incubator, or a patient on oxygen suddenly can't breathe? Unfortunately, we can't rely upon the local utility for electricity the way we do in the States. Because of this, we need to have a generator strategy.

The problem got worse when we discovered that the old World World II generator, the secondary backup for the three operating rooms and surgical recovery, couldn't support the brand new upgraded wiring infrastructure. So Paul brought out a spare generator that was in mothballs. After transporting it to outside the operating room building and connecting long wires to the electrical panel, it wouldn't start properly. After a half-day of working on it, Paul was able to get it to start and run, but it quickly burned out for some reason. That meant the only functioning generator was the small one that supports the maternity wing and its incubators, and that one was showing signs of crashing as well. Stress levels began to increase.

These three were bad enough under normal circumstances, but with the operating room generator not working, the situation became immediately critical. The major crisis, however, focused on the main generator. It had been functioning well until it was needed at about 9:30 Saturday night two weeks ago. I was sitting in my apartment when the lights suddenly started flickering. I'd not seen this before, and they went out completely a minute later. Concerned, I counted the 11 seconds in anticipation of the generator coming online, but nothing happened. I immediately got my shoes, bug spray, and flashlight, and headed out the door just in time to catch a ride down the hill with a worried looking Paul. Keir had barely beaten us to the generator building and had aimed his headlights into the generator area. They converged on the generator and began testing the system. We were joined shortly by two of the other surgeons and an overnight nurse from the hospital who helped hold flashlights and prayed in the background.

It took Keir and Paul until close to midnight to conclude that, unbelievably, three major components had failed, of which the main computer board was first. Paul had a new one on hand, so they swapped it out. No good. The motor would start but not stay on. Next, they started experimenting with the controls and became pretty sure the electrical voltage regulator had failed. Finally, they phoned an engineering specialist in the middle of the night in the States named Hannah who had visited a year ago to help with previous problems. Fortunately, she picked up and could talk. After going through some diagnostics, she became pretty confident that the voltage regulator was the culprit. Almost as an afterthought, they also determined that the alternator that charges the back-up car battery also wasn't working properly. This is a secondary problem, yet needs to be addressed soon.

Unfortunately, foresight can't realistically have every conceivable part available, and the voltage regulator and alternator needed to be bought and delivered. This is where working in the rural jungle becomes a major problem. Not only are replacement parts scarce in Africa and much more expensive than in the States, they are also only found far away from this remote jungle outpost. The best possible case was a supplier in Libreville, a day's drive away. The worst case would be to buy them from the States and ship them over, which would take weeks at best, more likely months. To make matters worse, Paul, Keir, and Hannah were not quite certain they had diagnosed the problems correctly. The only choice was to order the parts that were bad and pray nothing else was wrong. Stress levels rose even more.

By then it was midnight Saturday and the Libreville supplier wouldn't be open until Monday morning. We started praying that he would have the needed parts, that the correct parts would actually be sent (a common problem), and that there would be the means to deliver them here. Additionally, we prayed that the electric company would agree to provide us with power as much as they could for the next several days, especially during the day when the hospital was busiest. Keir drove to the plant on the other side of the river and explained the situation. He received a promise that the power would stay on during the day at the very least. Unfortunately, that promise was only as good as *their* systems. All four turbines at their plant were down and that the entire region was surviving on large utility company generators in towns 20 miles or more away. To make matters worse, entire towns and villages were without power much of the time. Stress levels became palpable.

Let's fast forward to Tuesday morning. The power had amazingly stayed on more often than not Sunday and Monday, especially during the day. It's humbling to realize how fragile an assumed part of life such as electricity can be. Providentially, the voltage regulator and alternator were purchased on Monday and they arrived first thing Tuesday morning via a delivery truck that had driven through the night.

The first sign of trouble was when Keir opened the box and found that the new voltage regulator looked nothing like the old one. Fortunately, the directions indicated this to be the new and improved replacement for ours. Unfortunately, its installation looked to be incredibly complex. Keir, Paul, and I headed for the generator.

When they were ready to start, we prayed first. We prayed for God's guidance, for wisdom and clear thinking, and that no mistakes would be made to set us back even further. I really like this intentional reliance on God! From 9:30 until 2:00 that afternoon, they painstakingly deciphered electrical diagrams, re-engineered how to mount the new 10-by-18 inch regulator onto the frame of the generator, and carefully connected and double-checked wire after seemingly endless wire. Finally, only one critical question remained: For how much voltage was the generator rated? The final two wires depended on this answer and a mistake at this point would fry the whole system. Keir and Paul looked everywhere and couldn't find the answer. We looked at our watches — it was early morning in the States. They decided to wake up Rod Lanser, the electrical engineer who I'd traveled and worked with the first two weeks here. Fortunately, he was awake and definitively answered the question; the last wires were connected.

The moment of truth had arrived. We stopped and again prayed, this time for God's favor. They had done everything humanly possible; the rest was up to God. After one last soul-searching eye contact and a final deep breath, Paul turned the switch. The generator came on and functioned perfectly! We celebrated like we'd just won the championship. After another hour of testing and monitoring, they declared victory. It was very emotional for each of us. What an honor to be part of something so meaningful to so many people.

The bottom line is that without the teamwork and relationship between Paul and Keir, this repair never would have happened. By themselves, neither man had the knowledge or skills to complete it without the other. The repair took all of their combined individual strengths, as well as an amazing level of patience and trust in each other. It's truly amazing what God can do when two people set ego and cultural norms aside to work for a higher purpose.

Lessons Learned So Far

1. Paul and Keir are great reminders not to judge someone based on what they do for a living.

2. Synergy and teamwork produce better outcomes than working alone.

3. Holding flashlights, handing tools, and being a gofer for Paul and Keir were important roles, even though I didn't do much more than that. I joked with Keir that I was now ready to be an operating room assistant!

4. Intentional reliance on God is a great habit.

To Ponder

Who in my life can I call an "eclectic partner"?

Affirmation

*I seek out different and complementary
people who help me grow!*

Not Everyone Makes It

A man died in front of me today. While it's true that many people recover at Bongolo Hospital thanks to God's presence, the reality is that not everybody lives. This afternoon, Joures ('Juress') and I were working on non-functioning lights in the Emergency Room building. We had just positioned the ladder to work on the next fixture, but before Joures could climb the ladder, a crisis broke out behind the curtain in the patient room right in front of us. It was immediately clear a person was suddenly in a life-and-death situation. Very quickly, we folded the ladder and moved out of the way. Seconds later, Dr. Renee Valach rushed in from another part of the hospital and took over from the nurse. She was followed by a new nurse's aide and a nurse, as well as eight family members and friends. ER access rules at Bongolo are more flexible than back home.

After about 10 minutes, Joures and I prepared to leave the building, when Renée called out, "Doug, is that you?!" I pulled back the curtain and she laser-beam stared into my eyes and asked me to go get a monitor from her office in the next building. I nodded, "Yes" and was on my way. I prayed God would help me get there because I'd only been to her office once and there are a lot of buildings. Fortunately, I found it on the first try, but there was no monitor where she said it was. As I was frantically scanning the room, one of the ER nurses came in. He couldn't find it either. I pointed to a small device that resembled a monitor that might be the right one, but he said it wasn't. I left it there and we ran back to the ER. I told Renée I couldn't find it, that I didn't know what to look for. She pointed at a small monitor over her head and said it looks kind of like that one. It was just like the one I wanted to bring.

I ran back, nearly pushing my way through the gathering throng of family and friends, grabbed the machine and its cords, and sprinted back. As I slid through the people and into the patient's room, I called out, "Here it is!" Renée looked up from hand pumping oxygen into the man's mouth and said with a somber expression that she didn't need it any more and to put it on the floor. The air went out of me, as well. I did as she instructed, then slipped back out. I moved to the other side of the room and prayed. More and more family came and went. Cell phones rang. I watched as Renée and her team administered CPR, and injected adrenaline and other medicines. Nothing worked. His pulse, as displayed on the monitor, slowed each time she paused.

Twenty minutes or so passed, and there was no progress. He was gone. After declaring him dead, Renée did a few other things. While she did, the traditional Gabonese wailing and crying immediately began as more and more people flooded in and out. I stood there, silently praying, then made my way to the door. She looked up, for some reason caught my eye, and gravely shook her head. I was flooded with all kinds of emotions. I didn't know the man and hadn't been part of his story until a few minutes earlier, but I fought back tears. I felt sad, helpless, and numb. I'd done everything I could, but still felt like I'd been in a losing fight. I wondered if it would have made a difference if I had brought the correct monitor. In my gut, I knew that was ridiculous, but the implications of what just happened were hovering there, just the same.

The last time I'd felt this way was when I witnessed someone die over 20 years earlier. My family and I were living outside of Pittsburgh in Avalon, PA. Our home was on the main street, and directly across from us was a small but nice four-story senior citizen independent-living building. Like our home, it was quite old, made of brick, and carved into a typical Pittsburgh hillside. That day, I was out in my front yard and I glanced up to see an elderly man, who was already having trouble walking, attempt to go up the sidewalk. For some reason, he made a sharp left and took a step up the even steeper grassy portion. I watched as he tottered. As he started to fall backwards, I bolted across the street as fast as I could, but I was too late. He fell straight backwards and I heard his head hit the concrete; it sounded like a melon breaking. I reached his side yelling for someone to call 911, but by the amount of blood oozing from the back of his head onto the sidewalk, it didn't look good. I tried to pray and talk with him about Jesus, but I'm not exactly sure what came out of my mouth. A couple of minutes later, an ambulance arrived, but it was too late. He passed quietly away. I was stunned; it had happened so quickly. I've kept a close eye out for tottering people ever since.

I never got any more information about him. It's interesting that God provided the answers I needed today that I didn't get many years ago. I was just getting back to my apartment after work when Dr. Izzi and Joanna Thelander came past on their regular workout. After quick greetings, I told them I'd seen my first person die here. Izzi nodded and told me he was the principal of the big high school in Lébamba, and that his dying was really tragic. I thanked them. A few minutes later, I'd changed into running clothes and had made it to the bottom of the first hill. I figured a run might help.

As it turned out, one of the African surgeons I've gotten to know "just happened" to come walking up the hill toward me. I stopped and asked him what he knew about the man's death in the ER today. We walked together part way back up the hill and Elysée ('Ellisay') told me that the patient had been brought to the hospital yesterday in a coma. He had suffered a massive stroke at home, likely a direct result of not faithfully taking his blood pressure medicine. I thanked him for the information, breathed a sigh of relief that I'd somehow not killed him, and continued on my way.

Later, Dr. Renée filled me in even more. The man's problem was kidney failure from untreated, severe high blood pressure. Because his kidneys didn't work, fluid built up in his lungs so he couldn't breathe. Renée informed me that she had been about to ask me to help with chest compressions right before more help arrived in the man's room. She remembered I'd been a lifeguard. "Wow," was all I could think.

Besides death, another perspective of "gone in the blink of an eye" is that some chances to lovingly serve others are like what I had experienced that day – flashes of opportunity that are here and gone in a second. If we don't jump on them instinctively, it's often too late. While I don't have any medical training, I celebrated that I jumped in as best I could, both with the old man and here today. My goal is to love and live like Jesus wants me to, with all-out commitment. I tried my non-medical best to help both men. Sadly, neither attempt resulted in a longer life for either of them. The good news is I'm not kicking myself for not doing more. I'm celebrating that I did all I could with what I had – I'd responded in a time of need. Every day, I'm working to respond better and faster to those opportunities to serve.

Any of us could die today. Like these two men, we are fragile beings in spite of what our egos tell us. I recently read a humorous piece about a 40-year-old who said he felt like a 20-year-old until he hung out with 20 year olds. Then, he felt like a 40-year-old! I can relate to that. We may feel indestructible, but any of us could be gone from this world in the blink of an eye. Truth be told, I'm excited to one day get to heaven because of my faith in Jesus as my Lord and Savior, not because of my actions. One of my hopes is to get a big hug and hear God say to me, "I'm proud of you. Your life was awesome!"

Lessons Learned So Far

1. It's enough to do all I can. It would have been easy to beat

myself up in both of those situations because I didn't have any medical training beyond Boy Scout merit badges and lifeguard first aid, but I didn't. I did what I could.

2. Jumping at the opportunity to help someone is its own reward. Be spontaneous and generous. It's the stuff that makes life worthwhile.

3. It's permissible to be upset when something terrible happens, especially when it's right in front of you. Tears are okay.

To Ponder

How enthusiastically am I living right now?

Affirmation

Adventures with God are my everyday experience!

Note: You've got to read Bob Goth's great book, *Love Does*, of stories and life lessons that spur us on to live a life of no-holds-barred, no-regrets, all-out giving and loving. It's a quick, powerful read.

Observations & Experiences Part 2

I'd like to share some observations about the local people. I find it interesting to look for similarities to back home, as well as to absorb the sometimes striking cultural differences. When discussing this, it wouldn't be accurate to simply say Gabonese because this area is quite a melting pot of other central African countries, especially Mali and Senegal. The other thing I need to be careful of is that I've only been here for a couple of months. There's no way I can know this culture in any real depth. Finally, Bongolo is a rural, jungle hospital and the people around here are rural, small-town folk. I have absolutely no idea what the differences a city would hold.

With that said, here are some thoughts about local people, places, and things. How many similarities and differences do you see in American life? Your own life?

- People here are very image conscious. Most wear their better clothes out in public, whether shopping, at the hospital, or visiting.

- Men traditionally wear long dress slacks and a long-sleeved shirt. I don't know how they stand the heat, but I guess if you grow up here, it's all you know! Men *always* wear long pants unless they are playing sports.

- I've only seen a few Muslim men in traditional clothes; all of the rest of the men are dressed "Western."

- Most women over 30 years old wear colorful, full-length skirts or dresses, with matching headwear.

- Both the male and female dress codes are changing with the younger generation, unfortunately. They are becoming more Westernized. Younger men and boys wear jeans and t-shirts, and some of the younger women and girls wear skinny jeans and tights underneath a skirt.

I'm more traditional, I guess, as I like the dressier look.

- Most of the Western clothing looks as if it has come from thrift stores, probably from Europe. That's not a judgment statement, for 90% of my clothing comes from thrift stores. Years ago, I figured out I could have a fantastic wardrobe at a fraction of the cost. That's buying from a First World thrift store, however. Back home, I've often seen bundled "bricks" of clothing at the back of my big thrift store — stuff they can't sell — and wondered where it goes. Now I know: It's sold to distributors in Third World countries. It makes me sad, but I have to admit, the quality is better than locally-made clothing.

- I have only seen one or two people smoking, and that was in Lébamba. None of the stores I've been to have a cigarette section like at an American store. While I've been thrilled not to smell burning tobacco, I'm guessing so few people smoke due to poverty rather than common sense.

- Alcohol is a problem in the villages and in Lébamba, like most places. The big food store has an entire alcohol aisle and there are lots of tiny "house bars" where they sell beer and maybe some liquor. I haven't been in any; it's not the missionary thing to do.

- I've been thrilled not to have seen any tattoos, except on the upper back of one of the resident (student) surgeon's wives. Yes, she's American.

- I can't tell if the local construction workers swear — my French hasn't gone in that direction! They can be loud with each other, however, tease a lot, and look at passing women (no hooting, however).

- The Gabonese are very susceptible to malaria, the number one killer in Gabon, because they don't take daily anti-malaria medicines like the missionaries and I do. It is too expensive for most.

- There's a stereotype of "the lazy Gabonese" that I've been trying to unravel. Their reputation is that they don't work hard and are not entrepreneurial at all. I've talked with a number of people and have come up with at least three possible explanations. The first is that Gabon is relatively wealthy due to oil exports – amazingly, it is OPEC's smallest member. Decades ago, the government began handing out oil profits to every adult, similar to Alaska's oil program. The following generations have grown up not needing to work very much because of their reliance on the government's generosity. The second reason is Gabonese value relationships and personal image over nearly anything else. If you have money and a relative asks you for it, it is expected you will give what you have. I thought this was absurd, but then I thought about life back home where the same can be true. A possible third reason is that some people do just enough to get by. It all sounds hauntingly familiar.

- There are a number of other larger employers around, but Bongolo Hospital is by far the largest. Many people work on farms, at schools, for the government, or for various small businesses. I wish I had time to learn more.

- Many people get most of their food from subsistence farming, and purchase the rest with their government check, and whatever other work they can get.

- Most of the construction laborers are paid about $1 per hour. I don't know what others make.

As I've noted all of the above and more over the last couple of months, I can't help but reflect on how many of these issues remind me of home, just packaged differently. Parts of the First World are no different than here.

Lessons Learned So Far

1. Intentionally looking for interesting details is fun.

2. It's easy to compare and judge, both positively and negatively. I need to guard against this.

3. I learn an awful lot by asking questions and then listening. Because of this, I find I do a lot less talking than I used to.

4. While I'm happy people here have decent clothing, I'm saddened both that they are losing their cultural identity to more Western ways, and also that what they're wearing is made up of thrift store cast-offs.

To Ponder

*How much attention do I pay to
the people, places and things in my life?*

Affirmation

Curiosity is a lot of fun!

Observations & Experiences Part 3

Here are a few more people, places and things I've observed and pondered, in no particular order:

- The Gabonese at first appear to be very reserved. Almost everyone absolutely lights up, however, when I wave at them from the truck or nod and greet them in French or Nzebe, the local tribal language. Yes, I've learned a little Nzebi!

- Gabonese people out and about seem to walk very slowly. Is it the extreme heat or because they think they have nothing important to do?

- Native men stop and pee on the side of any road whenever the need comes upon them. It almost doesn't matter where or who's around.

- I'm not sure where the women relieve themselves and haven't had the courage to ask.

- Native women and girls spit a *lot*. I don't remember seeing a single man spit.

- Gabonese cannot pronounce "th" when trying to speak English. For example, "the" comes out three or four different ways! It is interesting that there is no corresponding sound in French or Nzebe.

- My friend Antoine and I laughed and laughed as he valiantly tried to pronounce "three" He got me back with a similar French word I could not pronounce.

- It is pretty normal to see locals cooking over open wood fires. It's also normal to see mostly women canvassing for wood to burn, and the sight of them makes me feel First-World badly. At the Station homes, our gas stoves are converted to use butane tanks, a cousin of propane.

- Small numbers of chickens, goats, and sheep wander everywhere, except for the Hospital compound.

- Sheep do not have fluffy wool here; they look just like the little goats. In fact, they're initially almost impossible to tell apart.

- I've been told there are two ways to tell sheep and goats apart. One way is that a sheep's ears point down and goat ears are up. The second is that sheep tails are always down and goat tails are always up. I think the second way is the accurate one.

- The dirt everywhere is a rusty red. Most of my clothing and all of my shoes are now tinted this color.

- The Gabonese I've seen so far all look well fed. I'm not sure, however, that their nutrition is well balanced. The typical person eats a lot of bread, rice, and manioc root to feel full. I haven't been able to figure out if Paul's men eat during lunch. They disperse and do their own thing.

- Gabonese skin has a faint brown-reddish tint to their near black coloring. It's very different from anything I've seen, and I like it.

- I sensed some Gabonese attitudes at both Lébamba and the Hospital that are similar to some inner-city entitlement attitudes I've been around.

- There is no government support system, such as food stamps, so families take care of each other. For example, it is culturally expected that if a family member asks for money, it is to be given to them, even if the asker is taking advantage of somebody.

- The only acceptable way I've heard so far to not give money to a family member is to invest it over a period of perhaps decades into building a retirement house into which they will eventually move. Because of this, partially-finished homes are everywhere and hardly anybody has cash on hand. When I first arrived, I thought those half-finished houses were in ruins and should be torn down. It goes to show how wrong it is to assume anything, especially in a foreign culture.

- The Gabonese are great singers. Everything I've heard about African singing is true.

- I've only seen a couple of bicycles and very few motorcycles.

- Very few people own cars, and the cars, SUVs, trucks and minivans I've seen are nearly all older and beat up. Considering the rutted-dirt roads and limited mechanics, that's no real surprise. You can imagine my surprise at seeing a gorgeous, clean, new black Mercedes coupe the other day.

- "Mass transit" is made up of a loose system of individually-owned cars, minivans, and SUVs called taxis. They are more like buses than taxis because they follow specific routes. Unlike American buses, however, they only depart when they are full to overflowing. The old "clown car" analogy would be pretty accurate to describe what they look like.

- I haven't been able to determine if there is an official taxi ownership system. There is certainly nothing like a Yellow Cab brand.

- Local construction laborers are similar to U.S. construction workers with far fewer power tools.

- Many of the local workers look up and wave when I pass by. That's very different from back home. Maybe it's because I'm white?

- Nearly all of the shops and stores are owned and operated by foreigners. Also, nearly all of them are Muslims.

- Muslims are still a small percentage of the population in our region. For now.

- Shopping tip: When shopping for small items, it is traditional to say how much you want to spend and they give that value to you. For example, if I want to purchase little fresh-fried donut bites, I tell the seller I want 500 CFA worth (a little less than a U.S dollar) and I get a very satisfactory supply.

- Because of this practice, few of the street vendors in Lébamba have change.

- I've been pleasantly surprised that there is virtually no haggling as part of the shopping culture.

- At first, I wasn't certain if I was being taken advantage of by the street merchants. Prices sometimes rise if you're white, especially if you don't know any better *and* don't speak French.

- After my first street vendor shopping experience, I've made it a policy only to go shopping for fresh food items with a French speaker. The stores are okay because prices are clearly marked and they show me the total due on a calculator.

- The overall local crime rate is low. This city boy continues to be amazed that I can safely leave my key in the ignition, or leave tools and materials in the exposed back of the truck, even when in town. Maybe the small town rural atmosphere is the reason.

I wish I spoke fluent French (or had an assigned translator) so I could actually get answers to the questions these observations raise.

Lessons Learned So Far

1. It's really smart to hang out with people who know what the heck is going on, especially when you're new to a place or situation.

2. Rural small-town living has lots of benefits, including a sense of community, low crime rates, and people watching out for you to a certain extent.

3. Stereotypes don't have to be true. I came to Africa expecting to be 100% vigilant regarding safety. The low crime rate and total lack of racial or tribal violence in this region are wonderful. I have felt very safe since I got adjusted to the cultural differences.

4. People are people. The interesting thing is that as soon as I began to say "Hi" (in French, of course), the response has been consistently warm and a little overwhelming. I love feeling welcomed instead of like an unwanted intruder.

To Ponder

*How many of these observations
echo life in America?*

Affirmation

*I love to learn and observe over time
so I can get a full picture!*

Things I Will Miss

At the halfway point of this adventure, I took time to reflect on my experience to that point. I also jotted down things about the States I either missed or didn't. As I'm at the end of my time here, I'd like to repeat that exercise, this time from the perspective of leaving my new home at Bongolo Hospital:

I won't miss (but am pleased with how I've adapted to living with):

- Cologne de bug spray. DEET and I will not be on speaking terms until Pittsburgh's mosquitoes come out to play.

- Concentrating on not scratching new bug bites and applying tiny dabs of Benadryl.

- Intense sweating when doing anything physical. I've never sweated through my jeans before and now do so every day before lunch.

- The persistent motor hum of ceiling and box fans (thank God for them, though).

- Slow and inconsistent Internet.

- So many bugs and ants – and that's just inside my apartment!

I'll miss:

- The people, both locals and missionaries. I've been blessed to form many new relationships and the beginnings of likely long-term friendships. It seems our conversations have reached new plateaus and I'm leaving.

- Working with Paul Davis. I've learned so much from him.

- Leading Paul's crew of eight men. They've been a blessing to me.

- The unbelievably fresh, clean air. Only on the far western edge of Washington State overlooking the Pacific Ocean have I ever breathed anything so wonderful.

- The heat and humidity (I can't believe I'm saying this!). I've taken to this weather like a fish to water. Somebody pinch me!

- My incredibly healthy complexion, skin, and fingernails. I can't believe the change.

- Exotic bird songs waking me up every morning.

- The beauty of the lush, green jungle vegetation.

- The dramatic topography.

- The sound and sight of the river and waterfall just below the Station.

- Walking outside and picking fruit such as bananas and some type of oranges.

- Cutting down banana trees (that's how you pick bananas).

- Having a machete with me, as a tool and not as a pretend sword!

- The just now beginning opportunities to branch out into the local communities.

- Speaking French every day, even though it's baby talk for now. Between lots of practice, patient French speakers, and Google Translate, I manage to understand enough, as well as get my points across.

- The adventure of and work involved with living in the remote jungle.

I'm grateful for:

- DEET insect repellent (I know, I know...believe me, it's a complex relationship).

- In spite of a head full of sand (an inside joke among

Paul's crew when we do or say something dumb — it sounds better in French), I stepped back and allowed God to arrange every aspect of my life for the year prior to my living and working here for two months.

- How much my faith has grown since arriving at Bongolo.
- I can't say this often enough: the financial and emotional support of my family, friends, and church family. You made this possible!

I'm certain I'll think of more as I go through photos and my journal.

Lessons Learned So Far

1. Keeping a written log of things as they happen is a great exercise for everyday life. I wonder how many God-moments I've promised to remember over the years but have forgotten?

2. Reflecting on how I've changed fuels my future growth.

3. It's amazing how easily I've settled in here in spite of major First and Third World differences. I'm pretty sure there are two reasons for this. The first is I'm where God wants me to be at this point in my life. And the second is that I had enough time to mentally and emotionally prepare as best I could to enjoy the differences. I'm starting to do the same in reverse as part of getting ready to head home.

To Ponder

*How would I answer these three
questions in my life back home?*

Affirmation

*My heart and mind are centered
on where I am right now!*

A Day of Goodbyes

My last day at Bongolo fell into three categories: church and brunch, final packing, and goodbyes.

Today is Palm Sunday, and I worshipped at the main Bongolo church, the same one I attended our first full day here. Instead of feeling overwhelmed, I was relaxed and content to sit on the hard, termite-eaten wooden bench. My friends, Dr. Sam and his wife Amanda, and I went together, and Sam periodically translated the French, for which I'm deeply appreciative. Time flew and, before I knew it, the two-hour service was over. After stopping to borrow a scale from the hospital (so I could weigh my luggage), Sam invited me to have lunch with them and some other resident doctors a bit later. I said, "Yes, thanks!" and headed home to continue packing.

I couldn't believe how big of an exercise final packing was. It proved to be a lot more time intensive than I thought it would be because I was taking back more than I expected, mostly gifts. Fortunately, I had planned before arriving to leave nearly all of my clothing, work boots, flash lights, safety glasses, gloves, and the like, for Paul's guys. I carried them over to the garage and placed them on my seat where we all meet every morning for prayer and work assignments. They don't get access to First World items very often, so I know this will be a blessing to them. Thank you, Sally, for turning me on to this concept! This was as much of a blessing for me as I hope it will be for the men. Regarding packing, I want to remember to bring the next larger size suitcase next time.

A second surprise blessing was the act of clearing leftovers out of my refrigerator. What started as pure drudgery turned into great joy. Two families had invited me at the last minute to meals, and I was able to give away several complete and partial meals, as well as leftover items, such as the last of my cheddar cheese, which went to Drs. Zack and Jen. It almost felt like a mini fishes-and-loaves experience because it seemed like the food in my fridge was multiplying. A lot of it was left-over local cooking, so the natural recipient was my Gabonese neighbor, Christine, who works in the hospital's accounting office. She was thrilled! The more American food items ended up with a few of the missionaries. The rest of my Seattle's Best decaf coffee and dried mango went to Izzi and Rene. I love to give things away.

The rest of the day, until close to 11:00 PM that night, was spent visiting my friends and dropping off thank you cards. Each person on the Station has impacted me differently, and I thought it was important to tell them how God worked through them. These rolling goodbyes started after church with Dr. Sam, Amanda and two-year-old Bela. They had welcomed me into their family and reminded me of the power of open-handed generosity.

I found Drs. Zach and Jen, with two-year-old Caleb, on their way back to their house and thanked them for sharing their story with me over meals, leading the jungle hike, and for offering some logistical strategies on how God could bring me back to Bongolo in the future.

Siko (a pastor and head of the hospital's laboratory) and his wife, Delphine (surgery recovery nurse), were next. They were another example of acceptance and love. Between the three of us, we could communicate pretty well. Delphine had been bringing me Gabonese meals for the last couple of weeks, and it was with great joy that I gave Delphine back her Tupperware along with an over-sized jar of unopened peanut butter I'd brought with me on the well-meaning advice of a friend who was concerned I wouldn't get enough protein.

I finally got that hug from Dr. Izzi, who impacted me beyond my ability to express when she asked me to help a dying mother and her unborn child by donating blood. She also made it possible for me to meet with the two of them two weeks later for a short conversation and a couple of photos. The four of us will be forever be linked. Also, Izzi included me in some internal missionary team activities, which I really appreciated. I hope to connect with her when she visits Pittsburgh this summer during her home assignment.

Dr. Renée wasn't home, but we had pretty much said goodbye after she, Izzi, and I played cards until late the night before. Renée got me involved with her attempt to save the life of the high school principal ten days earlier, and that experience opened wider the door to friendship. I felt God used me even though the patient passed away right in front of me. She's also going to be in Pittsburgh in the fall for advanced ultrasound training.

Ophthalmology resident, Dr. Bintu Peterson, and Rob, her pilot husband, have become soul-mates in only a short period of time. Rob was in Cameroon servicing the airplane, so I emailed him, instead of talking in person. Bintu and I chatted while she was getting her hair done on her front porch, and we laughed for 20 minutes. She is a passionate, enthusiastic woman who makes you believe more in yourself just by spending time with her. One of her passions is the worship band and singers at Bongolo Church. She's preparing them for a concert in May and loved my idea of a future U.S. tour. I could see the wheels turning as she considered the possibilities.

I ran into Dr. Deb Walker on my way to the Peterson's. She has a wonderful heart and has devoted most of her life's work to Bongolo. I admire her loyalty and dedication. Her duplex-mate, Sandy Freeman, had left the week earlier for three months of tropical disease education at a university in Belgium. Sandy is one of the people who runs the nursing school, and she took it upon herself to teach me some basic French grammar. She actually made conjugating verbs a fun-enough experience!

Eric (Bongolo's CFO) and Dr. Wendy Hofman (eye

surgeon) and their three children (Esther, Ely and Hannah, ages 5, 3, and 1 respectively) warmly and repeatedly welcomed me into their home. I had dinner with them more times than anybody else, and the kids had started calling me, "Uncle Doug," which left me feeling good all over. My best memory will be reading Cinderella to Esther while she cuddled up next to me. I didn't mind the extra body heat and sweating in the slightest

Paul and Meladee were second to last. Both are wonderfully selfless, each in their own way. Meladee, in her role of helping visitors feel more at home, kept me supplied with canned and fresh foods and juices. She was always cheerful and made me feel welcome. What can I say about Paul? In spite of being joined at the hip for weeks, he never once told me to stop asking questions or kicked me out of the truck because he was sick of me. I'll never forget the clear or subtle lessons I learned from him, whether it was how to replace the pump on a washing machine, driving the backhoe, leading his men, or managing the expectations of everyone who has a repair problem. I can't wait for next visit so we can work together again.

My last goodbye was with Dr. Keir Thelander, the medical director and team leader. I'd said goodbye to his wife, Joanna, earlier in the week, but we kept running into each other, so we laughingly kept saying goodbye. As the head of the visitor ministry, she was my point person for lots of things. Their kids, Luke (13) and Sarah (11), also impacted me because they remind me of my kids, Tom and Katie, when they were that age. Joanna is in high gear as she prepares her family to move back to the States in May so Keir can assume his new responsibilities as medical director for all of the PAACS surgical training program throughout Africa. It personally makes me sad that they are leaving. It's clear that God wants him there, but Keir, along with Paul, are two of the human reasons I came to Bongolo in the first place, and it felt very natural to work with both of them. I like the way he leads and can learn a lot from him.

Keir actually came over to my place at about 8:30 Sunday night and, over coffee, we just talked for a couple of hours. It was super that he was able to unplug for a bit. One of several significant topics was his response to an earlier question, "How can ACAC (my church) contribute in non-financial ways to Bongolo?" His considered responses were encouraging and will be well-received back home. He also spoke into my life and shared his ideas of potential future ways I could contribute at Bongolo, which touched me deeply. We concluded our meeting with prayer. In fact, several of the other goodbyes involved praying for each other, a wonderful custom I'd like to take back to the States with me.

I think the goodbyes were as impactful on some of the missionaries as they were for me. We closed this chapter and left doors open for the future. I left feeling like I'd become part of the family.

Lessons Learned So Far

1. Taking the time to intentionally say goodbye to everybody individually conveyed the message, "You are important to me." I had thought seriously about napping, writing, or exercising as part of my last day, but I'm glad I pushed those other activities to the sidelines.

2. Writing out and delivering thank you notes will be part of my life when I get home. I've said I would do this before, but this time it will be different. Even though it took quite a bit of time, it was worth every minute.

3. Giving away food and personal items motivated me to clear out an embarrassing amount of excess at my house. Clothing, furniture, and accessories clutter up my home

and could be put to good use by others. I'm going to have a "come take things" event of some kind and then take the rest to a thrift store, or simply have it hauled away.

4. Sometimes I am surprised by things people will say when saying goodbye, things I needed to hear but never expected.

To Ponder

*How might I aggressively give things away
to people who need them more than I?*

Affirmation

I am generous and other-people oriented!

CONCLUSIONS
and EPILOGUE

Re-entry Into American Life

It's been just over one month since landing at Pittsburgh International Airport.

My good friend, Michael Forlenza, had picked me up at the airport that Wednesday night. We had intended to get a bite to eat, but my plane from JFK in New York had been delayed six hours. Instead of landing at 4:30 in the afternoon, I arrived at 10:30. Needless to say, he instead took me straight to my house, with a raincheck for Thursday evening. To my great pleasure, my calico puffball of a cat, Tutu, came running to the door. She remembered me! I have to admit one of my silly, more minor concerns about coming home was that Tutu would have forgotten me, especially with the wonderful care and attention she'd received from Genna Frederick, who house-sat while I was gone, and super-neighbor, Gloria Raymon, who might actually love Tutu more than I do.

What a whirlwind this last month has been! After a couple of days of sleeping, getting unpacked, reconnecting with my closest friends, and loafing around, I drove to my parent's in Hamburg, NY, about 20 minutes south of Buffalo. I was certain they wanted to see and feel that I was home safely and I was not disappointed. After spending two days with them, I headed back to Pittsburgh on Sunday afternoon to get ready for work to resume on Monday. I'm grateful that my clients waited for me like they had promised. Work and the busyness of life kicked back in, and I could tell I would have to work hard to retain the somewhat simpler lifestyle and slower pace I had gotten accustomed to.

It's been really interesting to go through the entire cycle of coming home. For the first couple of weeks, I was greeted with cries of, "You're home!" accompanied by big hugs. It happened on the street in my city neighborhood, at

Mom and Dad's church, at the local places I frequent, and, of course, at my church. I won't lie: I enjoyed the attention. As I expected, most people only wanted to hear the briefest story from me before going on about their day, but others actually wanted to hear stories and see photos. Things quieted down pretty quickly, but it was nice while it lasted.

As I said, a lot more people than I expected were interested in looking at photos and listening to stories about my trip. Thank God I'd spent so much time going through more than 3,000 photos, culling them down to about 100 to consider for a presentation. That was still too many, however, so I ended up pulling about 60 and built a PowerPoint slide show so I could tell the stories that seemed most interesting. I could also overlay several photos on each slide, which helped keep it to a reasonable length.

I had my first opportunity to use it the second Saturday after I got home, I threw a "Thank you!" party for the dozens of people who had prayed and the 45 individuals who had financially supported the trip. About 50 of them showed up at my home that night, and we had a great time. There were so many who wanted to see pictures that my efficiently thoughtful friend, Chris Renda, divided them into four groups and handed out numbers! I gave four slide shows upstairs in the colorful California Room where my projector and screen are. I thought they were about 20 minutes each, but I later learned that they were more like 45-50 minutes long. I felt badly I'd talked so much, but nobody had seemed antsy. Afterwards, I was exhausted but exhilarated. Since then, I have had two other "Thank You" parties. Both of them were more intimate than the first one and I experienced a totally different kind of enjoyment.

One of my most gratifying experiences has been the impact of coming home in April, tanned, 20 pounds lighter, and having the rest of my weight rearranged into better locations. I knew I was losing weight because my clothing fit differently, but it really hit home when I got back. People were astounded. I told them it was my jungle diet: no beer, very little sugar, continual sweating, hard physical work, and consistent exercise in high temperatures. Unfortunately, I've gained about five of those pounds back this month. Initially, I ate and drank everything in sight, then went back for more. That's finally slowed down, but the joy of easily available Western food overwhelmed me for a while.

While it's been generally great to be back in my First World life, there have been some surprisingly challenging adjustments. I had been warned about the emotional conflict regarding the disparities between Africa and America, so I was ready for that. But there were a few minor and generally light-hearted ones that I could not have predicted.

The first was how strange it was to no longer speak French. I easily interacted with customs and airport personnel, and found myself wanting to continue to greet people and respond in French after leaving Paris. There I was with my baby French and strange accent confidently speaking French like I expected to be understood. Fortunately (or sadly, I'm not sure which), this faded away after a couple of days. In fact, that led into one of my concerns that instead of continuing to learn more and more, I would lose the French I'd learned. It's hard to learn a language while immersed in English. Since I've been home, I've worked to keep this from happening, but my French class next month at the local community college can't start quickly enough.

I noticed the second shortly after leaving Bongolo: I was the slowest walker around. I was so slow that little old ladies were passing me! This didn't make any sense to me at all. At Bongolo, I was always having to slow down so I would not leave others behind. I ran several times a week and took long, hilly hikes every weekend. How could I be so slow now?

It took a couple of days, but I finally started to keep up. Soon, I was again faster than most of the walkers. What a weird experience! I guess the slower-paced, African ways had seeped into me unbeknownst.

A third and even funnier challenge is that I'm now the "cold one." I used to secretly put down people who got cold easily in the privacy of my thoughts. After all, I grew up in Buffalo, NY and never noticed if I was cold until my hands or feet went numb. In spite of that, it's interesting how quickly I adapted to Bongolo's 100-degree days with 100% humidity, whether it rained or not. Therefore, coming back to Pittsburgh mid-spring was a bigger challenge than I'd anticipated.

For example, during my first week back, I was sitting at an outside table at my local watering hole, the Modern Café, with two friends, Bill Pricener and Tim Maloney. It was in the low 60s, which is typical for this time of year. We'd been there about an hour, and I noticed that I was getting colder and colder, but they didn't seem to be affected. They were wearing dress shirts and comfortably lounging in their chairs. It was obvious they were enjoying the temperature.

I, on the other hand, had on a heavy-lined shirt over top of my dress shirt, and my hands were stuffed between my thighs in an attempt to keep warm. I finally broke down and asked, "Are either of you cold at all?" They looked at each other and started laughing, saying, "It's 60 degrees and it feels great!" All I could say was, "Oh nuts, I'm the cold one now!" We had a good laugh at my expense. It didn't help that it turned unseasonably cold, with snow, for a couple of weeks right after that.

On a more serious note, I've struggled with (and still do) how much I prefer the more focused, simpler lifestyle at Bongolo to my complex, fast-paced multi-faceted life here. I don't like having to answer my phone so much, let alone deal with all of the emails and text messages that are a typical part of my American life. I have tried hard to keep the cell phone put away for hours at a time, but I'm losing that battle. The pace of life here has caught back up to me.

Most significantly, I'm struggling to find the deep sense of significance and purpose here that I had at Bongolo. The continual "something's missing" sensation I sensed prior to leaving is back, and it's stronger than ever. Don't get me wrong. I have a great life. I make enough money and I believe I help people whether at work, church, or in my volunteer efforts. I have wonderful friends who love me, and nobody could ask for better parents and family.

I've noticed, however, that something is missing here for me. In spite of the hardships, loneliness, and challenges while over there, I never felt insignificant. I knew that if I didn't do what I needed to, the doctors and nurses wouldn't be able to do their thing, and that people could get sicker or die. It's not that I live an insignificant life here. I am experiencing the difference between living a good life here and a great one over there. It's not that I could not do so here, it's that I'm convicted I'm supposed to be over there.

Epilogue: The Next Phase

How can I explain the call of God? Ever since Dr. Izzi walked up to me with the question, "Have I ever asked you what your blood type is?" and I experienced the deep joy of being involved with saving two lives, I've been freed up to pray that God would use me as He sees fit. Since that day, I've felt His call to return to Bongolo to live and serve. The wheels have begun to turn and the process has already begun. In my humanity, I've already gone back and forth between excited, as well as scared out of my mind, more times than I care to admit. Regardless, I still sense the call of God on my life.

Because of this, I've embarked on two important courses of action since I got home. The first is that I've jumped into the Christian and Missionary Alliance pastor-training cohort I was to start back in January, but delayed for obvious travel-to-Africa reasons. The third class, New Testament Survey, began this past week and we meet in person every Thursday night; this class will go into June. Then, I'll have the summer off to catch up by taking the online versions of the first two classes I missed. The thinking behind this is that I sense, as do my church leaders and the folks at Bongolo, that I'm more called to step into a to-be-determined, pastor-like role than an exclusively maintenance one. That said, I anticipate having my hands red-African-dirt deep into construction and maintenance, but not as my primary focus.

The second is, as noted earlier, that I've enrolled in my first French class at the local community college. This begins within the month. In the meantime, I'm doing what I can to retain and build upon what French I learned at Bongolo. I also believe that a few months of focused, immersion language school training is in my future. My goal is to be conversant enough by the time I go back that I'll hit the ground running.

As I mentioned before, I can't tell you how frustrating it is to not be able to communicate much past greetings and chit-chat. I'm going to do everything possible to see that's not the case the next time.

This next set of steps are far more complex than the lightning-like, three-month chain of events that got me to Gabon this past winter. It was a lot to quickly plan and execute a two-month trip. Expanding this into a multi-year journey is a whole other deal. I can't go there emotionally for now. It's not time for the "how" portion yet.

But is this next phase really all that different? I don't think so. Prior to this first trip, I had said, "Yes" to an assignment that only God could have created and executed so magnificently. I knew this was God's plan because I never would have come up with the idea in the first place and then gotten so excited so quickly. Because it was God's trip, I traveled to a continent I never had any prior intention of visiting, eagerly began to speak a language I'd never studied, and dove into work in an alien, rural environment unlike any I had ever imagined.

So God and I now have a "deal" similar to the one we've had around me getting remarried someday, preferably sooner than later. He knows I want to return full-time to serve at Bongolo. On my part, I trust that He has my best interests at heart, regardless of how long it takes, and that where He places me, and what He has me do, will be perfect. I surrender that my destination may not be back to Bongolo Hospital, even though that's what I desire. I'm praying that God will, just like this first trip, make His plans for me clear by throwing open the doors and windows He wants me to go through and slamming shut the ones He wants me to avoid.

Like in John Stanko's humorous, "God, I'll serve you anywhere" exercise, I'm resolved to holding my arms wide open and committing that I'll go and do wherever and whatever it is, *especially* if it's to serve in the jungle of Africa.

My prayer for you is that you will trust God and surrender to Him for whatever He has for your life as well.

Doug riding shotgun on the short flight from Libreville down to Bongolo, pretending to fly the plane. Actually, he had been given strict orders not to touch anything!

Bongolo Hospital, the Falls and surrounding region as we first arrived.

The Pittsburgh work team and Doug on their last day at Bongolo. From left to right: Ray, Doug, Bobby, Barb, Rob.

Bongolo Falls. Part of the hydro electric plant is on the left. Missionary homes are on top of the cliff to the right.

The only bridge for many miles -
over the river on the way to Lébamba.

Bakary's tipped-over truck in the ditch.

Part of the team who dug out Bakary's truck that caved in
the road. Bakary is wearing the blue jumpsuit.

Paul Davis and Dr. Keir Thelander
repairing the main generator.

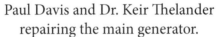

With the congregation of
Moutongo C&MA Church in Lébamba.

With Dr. Simplice Choba and Bakary Konate.

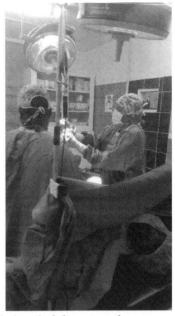

Dr. Elizabeth (Izzi) delivering the premature baby by C-section, with Doug's blood in the foreground.

Visiting the same mother two weeks later, with Amanda and Baby Naomi.

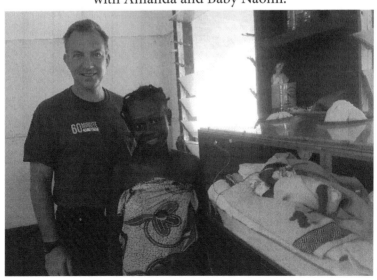

About the Author

The first 16 years of Doug's career was as a needs-based salesperson helping senior corporate executives solve their business problems. In 2002, in the midst of a tragic divorce, Doug sensed God's call to leave the corporate world; he did so and started a real estate development company. It became clear almost immediately that his "employee" mentality was inadequate to meet the intense needs and responsibilities of small business ownership, as well as life after divorce. This began a challenging and exciting journey of skill development and self-discovery. Since 2002, Doug has founded, built, and run four successful businesses. In 2012, Doug followed his purpose to facilitate change and became a certified life coach through Duquesne University. Doug currently operates two parallel businesses. The first is a life coach practice where he focuses primarily on the areas of becoming a healthy single person, especially as a Christian single. Doug's other business is a handyman company that spun out of his work as a real estate developer. Along with various board responsibilities and church-related volunteering, these eclectic ventures have honed Doug's skills and experiences to serve as a full-time servant of God both in the United States and in Gabon, Africa.

About Agape Africa Fund

All proceeds from sales of this book go to the Agape Africa Fund. This 501(c)(3) organization was started to meet the pressing life-and-death needs of the people in and around Bongolo Hospital. Located deep in the jungle of Gabon in central Africa, Bongolo Hospital provides Christ-centered, quality medical care to more than 40,000 people annually. On average, more than 2,000 patients and their families every year come to know Jesus as their Lord and Savior through the Hospital's ministry.

Agape Africa Fund collects and distributes donations of money, medical equipment, and general items to help people in need, both at Bongolo Hospital as well as in the neighboring villages. It also facilitates raising support for its identified in-the-field missionaries, of whom Doug Sprague is numbered.

The goal of this agency is to transparently and ethically utilize all donations for their stated and intended purpose. All donations are tax-deductible.

To learn more about our current projects, visit our web site at www.AgapeAfricaFund.org.

Made in the USA
Middletown, DE
29 November 2018